Introduction

The author of this excellent book, Dr. W. Herschel Ford, is destined to take his place among our most prolific producers and publishers of sermons. If this prediction turns out to be true, it will certainly meet with the hearty approval of his brethren in the ministry for, if I am not completely ignorant of what appeals to the average preacher, Herschel Ford's sermons are the practical, down-to-earth, well organized, effectively illustrated and homiletically perfect sermons that most of us constantly search for and are happy to have.

I have known Dr. Ford since our boyhood days in Georgia and have had him for revival meetings in every church of which I have been pastor. In some, my present pastorate, for example, he has been with me as many as three times. Thus, I have had the opportunity to see such sermons as are included in this volume put to the ultimate tests to which all our labors in sermonizing must come.

If it be true that "the proof of the pudding is in the eating," it is also true that the proof of the sermon is in the results following its preaching. In every instance, blessed and energized by the Holy Spirit, delivered by a man who has sought, above all else, to be a good preacher of Christ's Gospel, Dr. Ford's sermons come off with flying colors in the test of practical results. In revivals with my churches and with others of which I have had personal knowledge, there have always been many conversions, many additions by letter and many renewals of devotion to our Saviour. In every instance, when the visiting preacher had gone, the pastor was stronger with and much closer to his congregation.

But, to me, the real test of a preacher's genuineness and sincerity, the best evidence that his sermons are not just attractive arrangements of words, is what happens when he preaches at home, in his own pulpit, to his own people who have heard him a thousand times. Dr. Ford's present pastorate will do for an illustration. It is no reflection on many of us who have supplied his pulpit on various occasions to say that most of us are quite happy when three or four people respond to our invitations. But, when Dr. Ford preaches, it is a rare day that does not see ten to twenty, and, quite often, more, responding to his invitations and uniting with his great church.

So, judged by the preacher's homiletical standards, by the clarity and simplicity with which they present spiritual truth, by the tremendous crowds who go, Sunday after Sunday, to hear them and, above all, judged by the use the Spirit of God is pleased to make of them, these are good sermons, this is good preaching. In my humble opinion, they are the best we have had, thus far, from the fertile brain and consecrated heart of one of the great preachers of our time.

JAMES LEROY STEELE

Foreword

I am grateful to God for the reception given my previous books of "Simple Sermons." This volume is sent out with a prayer that these messages will be greatly blessed of God in introducing men to Jesus and in strengthening those who already know Him as Saviour and Lord.

Preachers and Christian workers everywhere certainly have my unqualified permission to use these messages in any way that will bring glory to our Heavenly Father.

W. HERSCHEL FORD

Contents

1

What Is Salvation

Neither is there salvation in any other: for there is none other name under heaven given among men, whereby we must be saved (Acts 4:12).

What does salvation mean? When we go to the dictionary we find this definition: "Salvation is preservation or deliverance from destruction, danger or great calamity." Here is a man who is drowning — he is going down for the last time. Another man leaps in, pulls him out and rescues him. This is one type of salvation. Here is a child in a burning building. The flames are encompassing the child. A brave fireman rushes in and rescues this child. This is one type of salvation. Here is a businessman who is about to lose all that he has. He is facing bankruptcy. A friend comes to his rescue with a gift of money and the business is saved. This is one type of salvation.

But the salvation which Christ offers to a sinner involves much more than this. A man who is lost and going down to death and hell cries out in faith to Jesus Christ. The Saviour reaches down and lifts him up and saves him from hell and eternal punishment. But salvation involves much more than this. It involves all that happens to a man from the time he trusts Christ until the time when he meets Him face to face in glory, and even down throughout the endless years of eternity.

I. SALVATION IS AN EXPERIENCE

In the old days the preachers spoke of "an experience of grace." They meant that something had happened between

13

God and the sinner. God and the sinner had met each other: the sinner had repented and had placed his faith in Christ, and God had forgiven him. If you have not had this experience you have never been saved.

John 1:12: "But as many as received him, to them gave he power to become the sons of God, even to them that believe on his name."

John 3:36: "He that believeth on the Son hath everlasting life: and he that believeth not the Son shall not see life; but the wrath of God abideth on him."

John 3:18: "He that believeth on him is not condemned: but he that believeth not is condemned already, because he hath not believed in the name of the only begotten Son of God."

Now, God takes the first step in salvation — He calls sinners. Sinners don't seek God; God seeks sinners. When the first man sinned, we hear God crying out, "Where art thou?" (Gen. 3:9). When Jesus came into the world He said, "The Son of man is come to seek and to save that which was lost" (Luke 19:10). Again He says, "No man can come to me, except the Father which hath sent me draw him" (John 6:44). In Romans 8:30 we are told that God calls those who are to be saved, then He justifies them, then He glorifies them.

What are these Scriptures telling us? Simply that God is the initial actor in the experience of salvation. He is the One who sends the Holy Spirit to convict; He shows us our lost condition; He draws us unto Himself. Jesus said, "And I, if I be lifted up from the earth, will draw all men unto me" (John 12:32). We are saved when we respond to that drawing power. We are lost when we refuse. Yes, God is the One who draws, who knocks, who calls.

> He stood at my heart's door 'mid sunshine and rain,
> And patiently waited an entrance to gain,
> What shame that so long He entreated in vain,
> For He is so precious to me.

When I was a boy and had done something wrong, my stepmother would sometimes say to me, "Just wait until your daddy comes home at noon." The waiting was worse than the punishment. I would always hurry through my meal, excuse myself and then go out of the house. But soon I would hear my father calling me, and oh, how it did hurt! He was calling me in to punish me. But when God calls a sinner, He calls him not to punish him, but to forgive and bless and save him.

Faith means trusting our small finite lives and personalities to a great Divine Being. This experience is the greatest experience in the world. When my automobile will not run, I take it to a mechanic, because I know nothing about motors. When I am sick, I go to a doctor, because I know nothing about medicine. When I need legal advice, I go to a lawyer, because I know nothing about law. But when I wanted to be saved, I went to the Great Specialist in Salvation, the Lord Jesus Christ. I turned everything over to Him and He saved me. He is in the salvation business; He is the only One who can save. And He says to every sinner: "Him that cometh to me I will in no wise cast out" (John 6:37).

Faith, then, is a committal of life to Christ. When I go into a plane for a flight, I trust myself to the plane and the pilot. I have faith that they will carry me through the clouds and storms and darkness to my destination. That is exactly what you do when you trust Christ. You trust everything to Him. You say, "Lord, I am a sinner, but You died for me. You tell me in the Bible that You will save me if I come to You. I do come now, trusting You to save me from my sins and to take me through the storms of life and bring me safely home to heaven at last."

In 1941 there was a great forest fire in New Jersey. Some soldiers were sent out to fight the flames. Eighty of these soldiers were soon trapped by the fire. But the pilot of a small plane which was flying overhead saw their plight. He flew down quite low and dropped a note to these men, telling them that he could see just one way out and that if they would follow him, he would guide them to safety. They obeyed him instantly — they followed him on the double-quick. He was able to lead them through the flame-lined channel to safety. Lost men are shut in on every side, but the Christ above sees their plight. He says to them, "There is only one way out — follow Me and I will save you. 'I am the way, the truth, and the life: no man cometh unto the Father, but by me'" (John 14:6).

Friends, He is the only way out. Have you had this vital saving experience with Jesus Christ?

II. SALVATION IS AN EXPRESSION

After the experience of conversion the Bible tells us to give expression to the thing which has happened in the heart by making a public profession of faith. Many people say, "I don't see why this is necessary." Well, on the Divine side, God has said that we ought to do it. On the human side, if Christ has worked a mighty change in our heart, if our sins have been forgiven and we have been saved, we will surely want to publicly profess our faith. Do you remember that hour when your wife promised to marry you? You were filled with a grand and glorious inner feeling. You didn't want to keep it to yourself — you wanted to tell the whole world. So likewise, if you have been saved, you can't keep it to yourself. You want the whole world to know that Christ is yours.

What does the Bible say about this expression? Listen to Romans 10:9-10: "That if thou shalt confess with thy mouth the Lord Jesus, and shalt believe in thine heart that God hath raised him from the dead, thou shalt be saved. For with the heart man believeth unto righteousness; and with the mouth confession is made unto salvation."

So you see that salvation is an experience in the heart and a confession with the mouth. Look at Romans 10:11:

"For the scripture saith, Whosoever believeth on him shall not be ashamed." If you are ashamed of Him, you may know that you have not been saved. If you are not ashamed of Jesus, you will certainly come out and confess Him.

Matthew 10:32-33: "Whosoever therefore shall confess me before men, him will I confess also before my Father which is in heaven. But whosoever shall deny me before men, him will I also deny before my Father which is in heaven." When I get to the end of the way, I am going to need someone to stand up for me. Christ promised that if I would confess Him here, He would confess me there. I want to hear Him say, "Father, he was not perfect, he was not always good, but he stood up for Me on earth and I will stand for him up here." When He says that, then I know God will say, "Welcome, my child, enter into the joys of thy Lord." But if I refuse to confess Him, if I deny Him down here, He will deny me up there. He will sadly say, "Depart from me, I never knew you." So you see that it is important to make a confession of faith. If you are genuinely saved, you will want to do this. You will not only confess Christ before men, but you will follow Him in believer's baptism and become an active member of His Church.

There are other times when we can give an outward expression of the salvation within. When a moral issue comes up we can stand and be counted on the side of righteousness. When people gather for worship we can express our feelings by being present. When we are called upon to support the cause of Christ with our means, we can express by a gift the love which is in our hearts.

Yes, in salvation we first have an experience in the heart — then we give an outward expression to this inner experience.

III. Salvation Is Exercise

If a newborn baby lies perfectly still and never moves, he will soon become too weak to live. If, after a person has been born again he never takes any spiritual exercise, he will remain a spiritual weakling.

There are several types of spiritual exercise. First, there is the private exercise of prayer and Bible reading. Jesus said, "I am the vine, ye are the branches" (John 15:5). If the branch is to grow strong it must have a vital connection with the vine. If you and I are to grow strong spiritually, we must have a vital connection with Christ, the source of all spiritual strength. This means that we will reach up to Him in prayer and He will reach down to us through the Bible. Prayer is man talking to God and Bible-reading is God talking to man.

You go into a telephone booth and leave the door open while you call a friend. While that door is open you cannot hear your friend and he cannot hear you. When the door is shut, you can hear each other perfectly. The world presses in upon us. The noises of the earth fill the air, but we can go to the secret closet, close the door, read the Bible and pray, and form a direct connection with God. Thus the soul will grow.

Then, there is the public exercise of Christian service. Most people think Christian service means teaching a class or singing in the choir. If you can do these things you ought to do them. But if you cannot, what then? You can do something else for the Lord. You can bring a neighbor to hear the Gospel. You can visit an absentee and tell him that you missed him at church. You can speak cordially to people at the close of the service. You can hand out bulletins at the church door. There are dozens of things which you can do for the Lord. In a certain battle a soldier became detached from his own company. Running up to an officer he cried out, "What must I do?" "Fall in anywhere," said the officer, "there's good fighting all along the line." There is no excuse for a Christian soldier to be idle. There is plenty for him to do in the way of Christian service.

We are moved to serve God by different motives, but the greatest of these is love. If we love Christ we will want to serve Him.

It is said that when the soldiers of ancient Persia went into battle they had to be driven by their generals. In the midst of the battle you could hear the lash of the whips goading them on to do their part. But not so with the ancient Greeks. They rushed into battle like hungry lions into a flock of sheep. What made the difference? This is it: the Greeks loved their country, their temples and their homes. They fought bravely because of this love. The true Christian serves Christ not simply because he fears hell or desires heaven. He serves because he loves the One who died for him and saved him.

So we see that salvation includes spiritual exercise.

IV. SALVATION IS EXALTATION

To exalt means to lift up, so we see that part of our salvation is the lifting up of Christ in our lives. Why is it that Christianity doesn't advance faster than it does? Why is it that so many people around us never go to church and seem to have absolutely no thought for spiritual matters? Could it be because you and I are not what we ought to be? Could it be that people do not see Christ in us? Could it be that they do not see any difference between our lives and theirs?

If you and I exalted Christ as we should, we would be so different that the sinner would say, "He has something wonderful within. He has something that gives him happiness and joy and usefulness. I do not have that something, but I would like to have it." I wonder if anybody ever looked at you and said, "He is a wonderful Christian—I wish I could be like him."

A Chinese Christian came to one of our missionaries and said, "I have learned to quote the Sermon on the Mount."

He stood before the missionary and quoted the Sermon perfectly, word by word. "That is wonderful," said the missionary, "how did you do it?" And the Chinese Christian answered, "I spent the last year trying to live it." We know what is in the Bible. We know how to live, but that is not enough. We need so to live that our lives will always show Christ to the people. The best sermon ever preached is that of a good life.

The Bible tells us that the Christian has two natures — the carnal and the spiritual. The carnal nature is the old sinful nature which comes from Adam. The spiritual nature is the one imparted to us when we come to Christ. These two natures carry on a continual warfare. When we feed the carnal nature with the things of this world, the carnal nature grows strong and the things which come from our lives are carnal and worldly things. But when we feed the spiritual nature upon the things of God, the spiritual life grows and those things which come from our lives are spiritual things.

An Indian, in speaking about these two natures, said, "In my heart there is a white dog and also a black dog and they are always fighting." Someone asked him the question, "Which dog wins?" And the Indian wisely replied, "The one that I say 'sic em' to."

A preacher got on a city bus, gave the driver a dollar and received the change in silver in his hand. He walked to the back of the bus and counted the silver and found that he had ten cents too much. Realizing that the money was not his, he went back to the driver and handed him the dime, saying, "You gave me too much change." The driver replied, "Yes, I know I did. I watched you in the mirror and I knew you realized that I had overpaid you. You do not know me, but I know that you are a preacher. I was just trying a little experiment. If you had kept that dime, I never would have had any more confidence in preachers." Someone is always watching us. What if we don't live like Christians every day?

We must live in a high spiritual altitude. We must live close to God every day. We should let every word and every deed be one which exalts Christ. Our lives are to be a silent witness, telling the world of the greatness and wonders of our Saviour.

V. Salvation Is an Extension

What do I mean by that? I mean that if you are a Christian, God will extend His hand of help down to you. When you come to pray in the name of Christ and according to the will of God, God reaches down a helping hand. When sorrow comes, He bends low to comfort, saying, "Let not your heart be troubled" (John 14:1). When you need guidance He says, "If any of you lack wisdom, let him ask of God, that giveth to all men liberally, and upbraideth not; and it shall be given him" (Jas. 1:5). When you have sinned and need forgiveness, He says, "If you will confess your sins, I will forgive and cleanse you."

God does not save us and then leave us to walk alone. He goes with us every step of the way. He says, "I will never leave thee, nor forsake thee" (Heb. 13:5). It is wonderful to be saved. It is more wonderful to have the daily companionship of the Man who saved us. We can lean all of our weight upon God. We can trust the everlasting arms. The One who made heaven and earth, the One who has all power, the One who can do all things, is ready to help us in time of need. So we see that salvation is an extension — it is God's extending hand of help to the believer.

VI. Salvation Is an Expectation

I have heard people say, "I have nothing to live for." That is certainly true of one who does not know Christ. But a Christian has something to live for; he is looking forward to something really wonderful. If this world is all, if we die and that is the end, it isn't worth the struggle. Paul said, "If in this life only we have hope in Christ, we are of all men most miserable" (I Cor. 15:19). Let us thank God for hope. As the mainspring is to the watch, as the sunshine is to the flowers, as the water is to the parched earth, so is hope to life.

Anticipation is one of the greatest things in the world. A young couple looks forward to their wedding day, happy in anticipation. A man looks forward to owning a new car, happy in anticipation. A family looks forward to moving into a new home, happy in anticipation. Anticipation is often greater than realization. The marriage may go on the rocks, the car may be a disappointment, the home may not please. But the Christian is looking forward to a life where there is no disappointment. He looks forward to seeing Jesus and his loved ones. He looks forward to living in God's heaven forever.

There are two avenues which lead to that Home Sweet Home. One is the avenue of death: one day you may say the last word, perform the last task, breathe the last breath, and then your eyelids will close in death. Your body will be buried in a casket. But if you are a Christian, your soul, your spirit, the real you, will soar out to be with Christ, redeemed by His blood. As Paul said, you will be "absent from the body, and . . . present with the Lord" (II Cor. 5:8). "For to me to live is Christ, and to die is gain" (Phil. 1:21). Oh, if you live for Christ, you gain everything when you die! Yes, death may come sooner than you expect it. Are you ready for it?

The other avenue which leads to heaven is the coming of Christ in the air. The Bible plainly tells us that He will come in the air to take up His saints. If we are still living at that time, we will never go through the experience of death. Listen to I Thessalonians 4:16-17: "For the Lord himself shall descend from heaven with a shout, with the voice of the archangel, and with the trump of God: and the dead in Christ shall rise first; then we which are alive and remain shall be caught up together with them in the clouds, to meet the Lord in the air; and so shall we ever be with the Lord."

A sign in Korea bore these words: "The precious blood of the gallant officers and men of the Seventh Cavalry Regiment has made it possible for you to be here." There are no such signs in heaven. But if there were, certainly one of them would read as follows: "The precious blood of the Lord Jesus Christ shed on Calvary's Cross has made it possible for you to be here."

What then does salvation mean? (1) It is an experience between a sinner and God. (2) It is an expression of faith in Christ. (3) It is exercising Christian service. (4) It is the exaltation of Christ in a good life. (5) It is the extension of God's hand along life's pilgrim way. (6) It is an expectation of better things to come.

When David Livingstone died in Africa, his body was sent to London for burial in Westminster Abbey. During his funeral procession, one of the greatest London ever saw, a shabbily dressed man pushed his way toward the front of the crowd for a better view. The people rebuked him for elbowing his way toward the front, but he said to them, "I have a right to see David Livingstone. I knew him better than any of you. We went to Sunday school together. But he decided for Christ and I decided against Him."

One man became a bum; the other man became one of the world's greatest souls. Friends, it makes all the difference in the world and in the world-to-come as to what you do with Jesus Christ. What is your decision? Don't you want this glorious salvation?

2

God's Remedy for a Sin-Sick World

> If my people, which are called by my name, shall humble themselves, and pray, and seek my face, and turn from their wicked ways; then will I hear from heaven, and will forgive their sin, and will heal their land (II Chronicles 7:14).

God gave Solomon the privilege of building the greatest building in the world, the magnificent temple of worship to Jehovah. When the building was finished the people came together for a great dedication service. When these inspiring services were over, the people went home rejoicing, thanking God for His goodness to David, to Solomon and to Israel. That night when the tired king went to bed, God appeared unto him, saying, "I have heard your prayer, I have witnessed all of the ceremonies and I have chosen this place as my house. But I want you to remember that if my people forsake me, I will send hard times upon them, and you will know the reason for these trials. I will not continue to bless these people if they forsake me, even though they have built for me this wonderful house." Then God in mercy says this, "When these calamities fall upon them, then, 'if my people which are called by my name, shall humble themselves, and pray, and seek my face, and turn from their wicked ways; then will I hear from heaven, and will forgive their sin, and will heal their land.'"

It doesn't take an eagle eye today to see that the world is in trouble and distress. In every paper we read that crime and trouble and violence are filling the world. We think of the "H" bomb; we think of the fear that fills men's hearts;

24

we think of the distrust of one nation for another and we come to realize that humanity has never lived in such uncertainty and distress.

Now America is at the heart of all this trouble. We have earned the hatred of the majority of the people of the world. We are in greater danger than any other nation. The Communistic forces of the world would delight to wipe us and our way of life and our Christianity off the face of the earth. Is there a remedy for the situation? Is there any way out? Is there any hope for America? Yes, our hope lies in getting back to God. Our hope lies in God's old-time remedy given in the text — in humility, in prayer, in seeking God's face and turning from our wicked ways.

We still sing, "God Bless America." He still wants to bless us. However, we do not see any great wholesale turning to God on the part of our nation. We are so far gone down the road of sin and pleasure and liquor and license and worldliness that we wonder if we will ever get back on the right track. Surely, only the return of Christ can straighten things out. But I believe this: Christianity is an individual thing and America is composed of individuals; so if we look upon this text as God's message to individuals, if we take it to our hearts and apply it to our lives, surely God will answer our prayers and bless our nation. The more of God's people who get right with God, the better country we will have.

I. We Are God's People

"If my people." There are more than two and half billion people in the world. They were all created by God, but they are not all His people in a saving sense. Many of them hate Him, others reject Him, and others ignore Him. Men talk today about "the brotherhood of man and the fatherhood of God." This sounds sweet and beautiful, but it is not true in a spiritual sense. We are brothers only if we are in Christ; God is our Father, only if we have come to Him through faith in His Son.

In John 8:44 Jesus is speaking to a group who claimed special kinship to God, yet they hated Christ and sought to kill Him. Jesus said to them: "Ye are of your father the devil, and the lusts of your father ye will do." It is true that those who follow Satan and do his works and reject Christ are not the children of God. Now how do you become a member of God's family? Well, you become a member of an earthly father's family through a physical birth, and you become a member of the Heavenly Father's family through a spiritual birth. Jesus said, "Ye must be born again." This is the thing that makes one a child of God. John 1:12: "As many as received him, to them gave he power to become the sons of God, even to them that believe on his name."

There is a vast difference between God's people and other people. God's people have trusted Someone other than themselves. They have realized their own weakness and have looked up to Heaven, trusting One higher and greater than themselves. God's people seek God's glory and not their own. The worldly man thinks of himself and his own interest; God's man wants to bring glory to the Father. God's people are serving God and not Satan. "He that is not with me is against me" (Matt. 12:30). There is no neutral ground. Are you serving God? If not, your influence is against Him and His cause. God's people are headed in a different direction. All men come into life the same way; they walk down the same road; they come to the same forks of the road. Some people take the upper road of faith in Christ and end in glory; some take the low road of the world and end up in eternal death. But God in this text is talking to *His* people.

II. We Are Called By His Name

"Which are called by my name." In the Book of Acts we read that the disciples were first called Christians at Antioch. The name was given to them in scorn. Their enemies thought that they were heaping insults upon them. Now this name is the brightest badge that anyone can wear. I wonder why these people called the disciples Christians. Surely it must have been because they reminded them of Christ. I wonder if you and I ever remind anyone of Christ. I am sure we want to do this. God help us so to live that others may see Jesus in us.

If you bear the name of Christ the world expects more of you. You must live up to this Name. Other people can do certain things and go to certain places and the world pays no attention to them. But the world expects more of a Christian. You must be careful how you live, how you act, what you say and where you go.

Alexander the Great had a soldier in his army who also bore the name of Alexander. But this man was a coward. Alexander the Great called him before him and said to him, "You must either live up to your name or you must change it." Oh, are we living up to the name that we bear, the name of Christ?

Adoniram Judson walked down the street one day and one man said to another, "There goes Jesus Christ's man." Can anyone say that about you? You have a great name if you are a Christian; it means that you are a follower of Christ. Do you remind anyone of Him whose name you bear?

III. What We Are to Do

We are told first that we are God's people, then that we are called by His Name; then He tells us what we are to do.

1. *First, we are to humble ourselves.* It is not easy for the average man to do this, especially the average American. We are a proud and boastful people; we take credit for everything; we leave God out of the picture. Our inventions are marvelous; our scientific discoveries are unbelievable; our standard of living is the highest of any nation; our luxuries are simply out of this world. And we did it all, we, we, we. To have all these things and to be humbly grateful to God is all right.

To leave God out and not to recognize that these gifts came from Him is fatal.

To humble ourselves means not only to confess our sins to God, but to admit that there is nothing good within us and that we can do nothing without Him. We are not to depend upon our talents, our brains, our ability, but altogether upon God. We are never to be puffed up or self-sufficient, or bigoted. All pride must go, pride of position, pride of possessions, pride of race or face or grace. We must renounce self and let Christ have the pre-eminence. We must say with John the Baptist: "He must increase, but I must decrease" (John 3:30). The way up to God is down. We must let go and let God have His way with us. "He that humbleth himself shall be exalted" (Luke 14:11).

There is enough to humble us. We take a look at the past and we see how faulty and faithless and fruitless we have been. We see how far short we have fallen of what we could have been. Then when we look upon all the blessings of God, surely we must cry out, "Lord, I have been a sinful person. Thou hast done everything for me and I have failed Thee. I am not worthy of the least of Thy mercies." Oh, let us acknowledge our failure and our need. Let us confess our sins of the past and our utter dependence upon God for the future. Let us humble ourselves in the dust before God.

2. *Next, we are to pray.* A boy fell one day and skinned his knee. By night he was in some pain, but not enough to bother a thirteen-year-old boy. Two days later he was worse and the family sent for the doctor. "I am afraid that we cannot save the leg," he said; "if it gets worse we will be forced to amputate it." When the doctor left the house, the boy called his brother Ed and made him promise that he would not let anyone cut off his leg. The boy stood guard at the door of his brother's room and the family turned to prayer. The mother and father and Ed took turns in praying,

rising from their knees only long enough to do the necessary work on the farm. The other brothers soon joined them in prayer. The doctor said that only a miracle could save the boy's life. On the fourth morning the doctor was greatly surprised to find that the swelling was reduced and that the boy was sleeping normally. In three weeks' time the boy was walking again. That boy was Dwight David Eisenhower. God had answered prayer.

He still answers prayer. Many of us are blackslidden and out of touch with God. We need to come back humbly to Him in prayer. Prayer means an approach to God, an appeal to God, an invitation to God, an expectation from God, an appropriation of God. What should we pray for? We should pray for God to reveal to us our need of Him, to reveal to us our sins, and to cause us to cry out for forgiveness and cleansing.

Where should we pray? We should pray in private, for "the effectual fervent prayer of a righteous man availeth much" (Jas. 5:16). We should pray in the family circle and in the congregation. But our greatest need is to shut ourselves off from all the world and really pour out our hearts to God. When should we pray? We should pray without ceasing, we should pray till the answer comes. Why should we pray? Because we need to bring God into our lives and this is the way to do it. Prayer changes things. Great things are wrought by prayer. We need to pray in order to get our hearts right with God.

3. *Next, we are to seek God's face.* Oh, there is where the rub comes in! The thing that hides God's face from us like the cloud hides the face of the sun is our sin, our worldliness, our indifference, our unfaithfulness. We must get the cloud out of the way.

It is by looking into God's face that we find the answer to our greatest needs. When we need salvation we read: "Look unto me, and be ye saved, all the ends of the earth"

(Is. 45:22). We look away from our sins and into the face of Jesus Christ and by faith we are saved. As we behold His face, we see what He is and we grow in grace as we seek to become like Him. As we behold His face we see One powerful enough and loving enough to supply every need. So, if we want the blessing of God upon us, we need to look away from all else and seek His face.

The Bible tells us that we are transformed by beholding. We cannot look into the face of Christ without being changed. A boy may do some awful things when his father is not around, but not when he is looking his father in the face. A man may be unfaithful to his wife when she is absent, but not when he is looking into her face. So the real Christian, looking into the face of Christ, wants his life to be clean and crystal clear.

God lives upon a high plane. Are you living down in the valley of sin and mediocrity? Then it will be impossible for you to see Hs face. Resolve, then, that you will no longer be content to wallow in the mud when you could be basking in the sunshine of God's love.

When you get a glimpse of God you immediately feel that there are some things which do not belong in your life and you want to get rid of them. When you once look into His face, you never again want anything to come between you and Him. So I plead for you to look into your own life. What is wrong there? What is it that hides the face of God? Is it some secret sin of the flesh? Is it some bad habit? Is it love of self, love of ease, love of money? Is it a critical, harsh, fault finding attitude? Is it some bad feeling toward someone else? Then won't you say as you sit in your pew: "By God's grace I will tear this thing out of my heart, so that I can look straight into the face of God again."

4. *We are to turn from our wicked ways.* If it seems that God is repeating Himself here, He is doing so to emphasize the fact that there is no blessing for you and me until we

stand in His sight with clean hands and a pure heart. This turning from sin is a natural result of a vision of God. The heart which has had its hunger satisfied by the sight of God's face will no longer want to hold on to the things that are abominable in His sight. The text says that we are to turn from our "wicked ways." Our way may not seem wicked to us, because we have been comparing ourselves with someone else. We have been saying, "I am better than he is." But when we come face to face with Christ, when we compare ourselves with Him, we are forced to cry out, "Woe is me!"

Anything in our lives which keeps us from being the very best Christians possible is "a wicked way" in God's sight. But when we give that thing up, we gain infinitely more than we lose. God never asks us to give up anything but something which is paltry and sorry in comparison to the riches He wants to give us in return. He just wants us to turn away from those things which keep us from being our best and from getting the most out of life.

Oh, beloved, seek God's face! And in the sight of His holiness, everything that is wicked and unchristian in our lives will melt away.

IV. WE ARE TOLD WHAT GOD WILL DO

1. *He will hear from heaven.* Aren't you glad that you serve a God who is concerned about you? When you try to do your best, when you turn away from sin and to Him, aren't you glad that He hears your cry?

A certain man commuted daily to his work in New York City. One morning the train stopped at an unscheduled stop, and the man saw the conductor running alongside the train toward the front. This man went out to see what had happened and found that a man had been run over and that both his legs had been cut off. The conductor rushed over to a nearby cafe and called for an ambulance. When the ambulance came, the driver was alone and he asked this man if he would not ride to the hospital in the ambulance with the injured man. He consented to do this, and the ambulance was soon screaming toward the hospital. The wounded man looked up and said to this other man, "Do you know how to pray? I am sure that a prayer would make me feel much better." "No," said the man, "I have never prayed." "Do you know one prayer that you can repeat?" "Well," the man replied, "I do remember one that my mother told me about. It was, 'God be merciful to me a sinner.'" The wounded man closed his eyes and kept repeating, "God be merciful to me a sinner." Then he opened his eyes and said, "I feel better. Everything is different. Something happened to me. I did feel all dirty inside, but now I feel that I am clean. I believe that God has heard my prayer and forgiven me. Why don't you pray that prayer?" About that time the ambulance reached the hospital. As the attendants lifted the wounded man out, he breathed his last breath, but went out to meet God with a smile on his face. The other man stood in the hospital waiting room for a while, looking out the window upon the city. Then he began to pray, "God be merciful to me a sinner." In telling about it later, he said, "God heard my prayer and saved me that morning."

Oh, yes, God does hear from heaven. In the text He says that if a poor backslider comes to Him humbly, praying, seeking His face, and turning from his wicked ways, He will surely hear. Don't think you have gone too far, my friend. God's love reaches to the depths, His arm is not short, His heart is open to receive you.

2. *Then God says that He will forgive our sins.* He is certainly a patient God. We sin over and over, but He says again and again: "Come on back to Me in true repentance and I will forgive your sins."

Robert Robinson wrote the wonderful hymn, "Come Thou

Fount of Every Blessing." Later in life he became worldly and backslidden. One day on a train he was seated by a consecrated Christian woman. She tried to engage him in religious conversation, but he was noncommittal. Without knowing who he was, she quoted this same hymn. It was too much for him. He broke down and wept, saying, "Lady, I am the unhappy man who wrote that song. I would give a thousand worlds to have the same joy now that I had then."

Have you lost the joy that you once had in Christ? It can be yours again. Stop right where you are, turn around, repent of your sins, and you will find God waiting with open arms to forgive you and plant His joy in your soul again.

3. *Then, God says He will heal our land.* Here is where the national application comes in. America is sick with sin today from head to toe. Only God can heal her, and this healing is dependent upon God's people. We are told that the majority of the people in America are Christians. If every Christian lived as he should, prayed as he should and voted as he should, we would throw out the evils of our land in a short time and God would heal America's sores.

Yes, God has the remedy for all of our ills. Are we willing to take the medicine? It will mean that we must humble ourselves and pray and seek God's face and turn from our wicked ways. And a great, loving, merciful Heavenly Father will do the rest.

In World War II a certain soldier's face was horribly disfigured. When he realized his condition he said that he wanted to die. The plastic surgeon told him that he could restore his face if he had a picture to go by. The soldier didn't have a picture, so he said, "It's no use, Doc, just let me alone." "But," said the doctor, "I can do something for you. Just pick out a picture and I will make your face like that picture." "It doesn't matter," said the boy, "that picture on the wall will be all right." The soldier did not know it, but this was a picture of Jesus Christ. The doctor performed the operation and it was highly successful. The man was greatly pleased when he looked into the mirror, after he had fully recovered. Then he said to the doctor, "Whose picture was that?" And the doctor told him that it was a picture of Jesus Christ. "What kind of a man was he?" asked the soldier. The doctor gave him a New Testament and told him to read about Jesus.

When the doctor came back a few days later, the soldier said to him, "There is just one thing for me to do. Since I look like Him, I have resolved that I must try in every way to be like Him." And from that day he was a changed man.

We are His people. We are called by His Name. May God help us to try to look and live more like Him every day.

3

The Church of My Dreams
Part One

> Christ also loved the church, and gave himself for it; that he might sanctify and cleanse it with the washing of water by the word, that he might present it to himself a glorious church, not having spot, or wrinkle, or any such thing; but that it should be holy and without blemish (Ephesians 5:25-27).

I have always been a dreamer. As a boy I dreamed of having great riches. I dreamed of having rooms full of gold to be used for any purpose. Later on I dreamed of power, of ruling many people, and receiving the plaudits of the millions. Later on there came the dreams of love and marriage and a home. Then I dreamed of success, of being a big executive, and of wielding power in the business world. But one day Christ came and called me into another life and all my dreams were changed. Now I have the high honor of being the pastor of a fine church, and all my dreams are for Christ's Church.

Often I sit quietly by day or lie in bed at night, and dream of what I want my church to be. Oh, if all these dreams could only come true, the world would look at my church and say, "There is the greatest church on earth!"

But churches are not made of brick and stone — these make the building only. Churches are made of men and women and boys and girls. Churches are made of human personalities and human brains and human hearts and human hands. Jesus Christ is the Chief Cornerstone. He is the foundation, and you and I are the smaller stones in the building.

Nothing has been built unless first it has lived in the

heart of a dreamer. The Temple in Jerusalem was a beautiful thing, but it lived first in the heart of Solomon. The Taj Mahal in India is said to be the most beautiful building in the world. A king built it for the queen whom he loved devotedly. He had dreamed of building her a beautiful palace, but she died before his dream came true. "Oh, beloved queen," he said, "I was not able to build you a palace while you were living, but now I will build you the most beautiful tomb in the world." So he built the Taj Mahal. But first of all this beautiful building lived in the heart of a dreamer. Every church, every building, every institution lived first in the heart of someone who dreamed.

But churches are not *built* on dreams. First comes the dream, then the hard work which makes the dream come true. God help us to dream our dreams for our church and to make them large, and then may God help us to work together as one to build a great church for the glory of God.

I. My Dream Church Is a United Church

You remember the old, old story of the father who had seven children, and who, through the lesson of the sticks, gave them a great truth about "united we stand, divided we fall." No church is strong if it is a divided church. Jesus said, "If a house be divided against itself, that house cannot stand" (Mark 3:25). If we are to present a solid front to the world, we must stand together as one.

A football team is composed of eleven men, but the men do not go in eleven different directions. They have just one object and they work together to get the ball over the goal line. An army may be composed of thousands of men, but they have just one object and they work together to overcome the enemy. If the church is to win, she must go out as *one*.

We sing the song: "Like a mighty army, moves the Church of God." Oh, what any church could do if all the members of that church would rise to the task that confronts them! We have seen the spectacle of a modern army conquering another country in a few days. If our church moved together as one always, we would soon be conquering great territories for the Lord Jesus. One drop of water on the beach does not cleanse the sand, but when millions of drops get together and the waves come in, they sweep the beach clean. One member may be influential in the community, but think of the mighty power of an entire church united in a common cause.

Sometime ago I went to hear a symphony orchestra of a hundred instruments. If each musician had played a different tune I would have heard a terrible noise. But when the leader lifted his hands, every man fell into line, and I heard beautiful music played in perfect harmony. If each of us church members plays a different tune, the church has nothing to attract the world. But if we listen to our leader, Jesus Christ, and follow Him, and all work together, the world will feel the power of the church. The world will be attracted by it, for nobody wants to join a divided church. So let's unite in the great purpose of the church, namely, to make Jesus known in the world. Let all of our giving and singing and teaching and preaching and work be to that end. Let us throw aside every prejudice, every difference and every jealousy and let us move forward as one great body under the leadership of the Holy Spirit.

II. My Dream Church Is an Attended Church

God knows the hearts of people, and He knew that they needed a place where they could meet for inspiration, fellowship and worship. He always meets man's needs, and so He planned the church. The Book tells us not to forsake the assembling of ourselves together (Heb. 10:25). God told us to go to church because He knew we needed it. No one has ever been hurt by going to church, but millions have been helped by it.

If you do not come to church, you do not learn what you

should. The church holds the highest ideals. You miss them if you do not attend. There are things in the Bible which you can never understand unless you come to church. You never know of the progress being made in God's kingdom unless you come to church. The Gospel is the best news in all the world, but you hear it not unless you come to church.

If you do not come to church your life is not complete. The most satisfying tasks in the world are found in the church. I tried other things, but I can testify to you today that I had no permanent satisfaction in my life until I became active in the service of God. How well do I remember that Sunday morning when my pastor and the superintendent of the Sunday school gave me a class of nine-year-old boys to teach. I found great joy in that class, and I have been finding joy ever since in the service of the King. You can never know that joy unless you come to church.

I want my people to love to come to church. Over in China a young woman found Christ as her Saviour. Her mother was a cripple and lived eighteen miles from the mission station. But this young woman took her mother on her back and brought her all the way to the mission station. She had a love for the church and she wanted her mother to find the joy she knew. And yet many of our people look for the least excuse to keep them from attending the worship services. We ought to love to go to church.

A young couple moved to our city. I went to see them and urged them to line up in the church, but they would not come. Months went by and then the man called for me to come to see him. When I went to the home I found the wife gone. The man poured out a sad story of sin and sorrow and disgrace into my ears. There was very little that I could do, but I kept on saying to myself that this disgrace could have been prevented and this sorrow could have been avoided if these people had lined up with the church and had lived according to its teachings.

I want my church to be an attended church, filled with people seeking solutions to life's problems, and under God I want to help them find solutions. I want to be the kind of preacher who will make them say, "I am hungry to hear the message of God as it comes to me through His servant."

III. MY DREAM CHURCH IS A FRIENDLY CHURCH

A church must have a personality. It must be friendly if it is going to attract people. There are those who ride many miles and pass by other churches in order to go to the church which is filled with friendly people. Someone said to a little boy one day, "Why do you go so far across town to church when there are churches very close to your home?" And the little boy answered, "I go to that church because they love a fellow over there." Oh, a friendly church will attract people miles away!

Bobby Burns, the great Scotch poet, one day was lonely and dejected. He drifted into a church and sat there through the services. Maybe he could have been won by friendliness but the members lost their opportunity. His life might have been different, but the members had paid no attention to him. Taking a hymn book out of the rack, he wrote these words on the flyleaf:

As cold a wind as ever blew;
A colder church, and in it but few;
As cold a minister as ever spak';
Ye'll all be hot ere I come back.

If you help to make your church warm and friendly you may be able to help many a man who might otherwise have gone down in the battle of life. The very one next to you may need God, and by your friendliness you may be able to win him. One man said to another, "What is the secret of your success?" The other replied, "I had a friend." Some day in glory someone will ask, "What brought about your salvation?" and the answer may be, "I had a friend. He invited me to his church. They were friendly and spiritual and in that atmosphere I found Christ." God help you to make your church a friendly church.

A woman came to our church three Sunday nights, and then said, "Not a soul spoke to me in that church." It was not our fault, it was her own. As soon as the benediction was pronounced she rushed out, and did not give us a chance to be friendly to her. Another woman said, "I found a wonderful welcome in this church, and I will be coming back." Please give us an opportunity to be friendly, and we will do our best to make you feel at home.

IV. My Dream Church Is a Loving Church

1. *They love each other.* In the New Testament someone said about the members of the early church, "See how they love one another." If we told the truth today, we would often say, "See how they hate one another." But we ought to love one another. We have found the same Saviour; we serve the same Lord; we have joined the same church; we are living for the same spiritual purpose.

One reason we do not love each other is that we do not know each other. We ought to do more religious visiting. To know some people is to love them. We would love most people if we knew them better. The Bible says, "Do good unto all men, especially unto them who are of the household of faith" (Gal. 6:10). Let's be one great family with Christ as the Head—a great band of Christians loving one another supremely.

2. *The members love the lost.* Why do we have a church? Simply that we might take the place of Jesus Christ in the world. He came down from heaven to reach out and to touch lives that were broken with sin, and to bring them to know the tender mercies of the loving Heavenly Father. That is why we are here. May God help us to love lost people. We cannot beat them into the kingdom; we must love them. Our hearts ought to go out to them in deep

compassion. We ought to love them and want to see them saved.

A Christian doctor went to China and built a hospital where he ministered to China's suffering people. One day the Chinese army marched in and the hospital was destroyed. What did the good doctor do? He followed the soldiers who had destroyed his hospital and ministered to their wounded. The leader of this army said to his Christian wife, "Why does this doctor do this thing?" She said, "There is only one answer. He is a Christian." The general humbly said, "If that is what it means to be a Christian, I would like to be one." In the course of time he became a great follower of Jesus Christ. Let's not stop to ask people who they are, nor what they are. Because we are Christians let us look through the eyes of Christ, and if we see the lost and needy all about us, let us love them for His sake.

3. *The members love the fallen.* Here is one who joins the church. Some of the church members watch him, hoping secretly that he will not hold out. If he does go astray they nod their heads and say, "I told you so." If a man falls into a ditch they kick him down deeper. If ever there is a time when a man needs sympathy, it is when he has fallen by the wayside. I want my church to be made up of people who love the fallen and who find their greatest joy in reaching down and lifting them up, and healing the wounds which the Devil has inflicted upon them. If we see one fallen, let's not talk about him and criticize him. Let us reach down to him the hand of Christian love and lift him back up again into the Father's arms.

V. My Dream Church Is a Spiritual Church

If the church is to mean anything to the world, it must be a spiritual organization. It may be wealthy, and it may have thousands of names on the roll; it may have a wonderful building; its crowds may overflow every available space; it may have the strongest preaching and the sweetest singing; but if it is not a spiritual church, it is nothing. The church is the only organization in the world which lays claim to having every object spiritual. We want all that we do to work out for the glory of God. A cup will not spill over unless it is full, and so unless we are full of the Spirit and love of God, our religion will not spill over and will not be a blessing to anyone else.

1. *If we are to have a spiritual church it must be a Bible-reading church.* Some years ago on the radio program, "Information Please," the experts were asked to give the first sentences of the Declaration of Independence, the American Constitution and the Bible. Without hesitation they gave the first two, but not one of the four great men could recite the first sentence of the Word of God. They were well read men, but it seems that the Great Book had no place in their reading.

2. *If we are to have a spiritual church it must be a Bible-practicing church.* What good is it if we know all the Bible and perform none of it? "Be ye doers of the word, and not hearers only" (Jas. 1:22). Many people can quote the Bible; they can even teach it in a wonderful way; but at the same time they have a wrong attitude toward others. We ought not merely to learn the Bible; we should live it.

3. *If we are to have a spiritual church it must be a praying church.* We ought to go forward, never with our heads up in the air, nor with our chests stuck out, but humbly on our knees. God help us to be a humble, praying church. Oh, what great changes would be made in our church, and in our homes, and in our lives, and in the lives of our loved ones, if we prayed more.

A Christian is more valuable than anyone else in the world, if in his life he reflects back the glory which is in Christ Jesus. If our church is filled with spiritual people, it will reflect Jesus to the world, and the world will feel the influence and power of our church.

VI. My Dream Church Is a Missionary Church

The works of my dream church are not only on this corner, but they must extend to the ends of the earth. We must have a world-wide vision of a world-wide task. We must do our part here, but we must also lift up our eyes and see the needs of the world, and go to the ends of the earth to supply those needs.

Everything in the world is largely missionary. Henry Ford was a missionary to the automobile world. His cars are now sold in every land. A great tobacco manufacturer once said, "I am going to put a cigarette in the mouth of every man, woman and child in China." The Gospel is a better product than either of these. We must take it to every man around the globe. We Christians in America are the result of Christian missionaries. The Bible and Christianity did not originate in any of our forty-eight states. The good things of God came to us because of the missionary spirit across the sea, and the church exists today in order that the good work may go on. Anyone is a missionary who has something to give to someone else, and is willing to give it. We are missionaries because we have the Gospel of Christ to give to the world—are we willing to give it?

An artist was once asked to paint a picture of a decaying church. It was thought that he would paint a tottering ruin. But instead he painted a picture of a magnificent building. As you looked into the open door, you saw the richly carved pulpit and the fine organ and the stained glass windows. But just inside was an offering box, and on the box was this card, "For Foreign Missions." There over the slot on the box the artist had painted cobwebs. That was the reason the church had decayed. She had forgotten others and had ceased to be a missionary church. Consequently she had died. Oh, I want my church to be a missionary church! I want her to love souls to the ends of the earth. I want her to follow Christ around the world, and bring those souls to the foot of the Cross.

How can we have this dream church? Here is the answer: Every member must throw sin out of his or her life, and that life must be dedicated wholly to the service of the Lord Jesus Christ. If even one member refuses to do this, our church is weakened just that much. Oh, God, give us a united, attended, friendly, loving, spiritual, missionary church!

A violin string lay upon the table. It was a helpless inanimate thing. There was in it no power, no strength, no beauty, no music. Then the master violinist came to the table and picked up the string. He fitted it into its predestined place in the violin. Soon he was turning the key and getting the string in tune. Then he touched that string with the bow, and brought forth lovely music from that which had been dead and inanimate before.

Many church members are lying idle like the string of the violin. Don't let your life be like that lost string lying on the table. Come and put that life into the hand of God. Let Him fit you into your rightful place in the church and its activties. Don't be satisfied merely to have your name on the church roll. Be a real Christian. Come and help your church become the church of our dreams, for the sake of Jesus Christ.

4

The Church of My Dreams
Part Two

I was glad when they said unto me, Let us go into the house of the Lord (Psalm 122:1).

If the church of Jesus Christ is what God wants it to be it is the most influential institution in the world. You may rear your buildings of commerce and industry; you may build your great schools and universities; you may lift your skyscrapers into the air; but none of these will have the influence of a humble church which is carrying out God's will in the world. But if that church is not working at its God-given task, it is failing in its mission.

The sensible person turns to the church in the hour of need. If you are feeling the burden of guilt, there you hear of a Saviour who can lift the load. If there is sorrow in your heart, there you can find the comfort and peace that passeth understanding. If you are lonely, there you can find the sweetest fellowship. If you are perplexed, in the quietness of God's house you can find the answer to life's riddles. If you are confronted with problems, in God's house you find solutions and guidance down life's pathway. You need to come to church and bring others along to enjoy its soothing ministry. There are hungry hearts all around you — life holds no satisfaction for them. They have tried everything else. How we do wish that they would try Christ and His church! There and there only will they find true satisfaction in this world.

It is good to see a church full of people; it is better to see people full of the church. It is God's plan for His church to be uppermost in our hearts and minds. We can enjoy the

45

good things of life and yet let the church be the center of all things. Oh, let us fill our hearts and minds and lives with the church! Let us dream our dreams and help them to come true.

I. MY DREAM CHURCH IS A PEOPLE'S CHURCH

By that I mean that it is a church which belongs to all people, where everyone feels at home, where every member feels that he is a vital part of the whole. Over a certain church door I saw the inscription, "The rich and the poor meet together here, the Lord is the Maker of them all." I want my church to be one where every member can say, "This is my church. I love it and am proud to belong to it."

Some churches are run by a few prominent members. In the ideal church everyone is a "main member," all have an important part in all of the meetings. The ideal church is one big happy family, living and loving and working for the Heavenly Father. In my dream church there are no old folks, no young folks, no rich nor poor, no big nor little — they are all just folks. They are all equal in the sight of God.

A great word in a good church is the word "fellowship." On some ships you have first-class, second-class and third-class, but on the good ship *Fellowship* everyone travels first-class. Let us keep this as the glory of our church, that all of our members are on an equal footing and that even the least of them is of great value to the church. If even one member feels that he doesn't have a part, and drifts away, the church is weakened just that much.

I went into a factory a little while ago where the men were not known by their name, but by a number. It is not this way with the Lord; everyone is someone in His sight. In an ideal bridge the load is evenly distributed over the entire structure. When a train crosses that bridge every piece of material bears its share of the strain. And so it is in a people's church. All of us want to share the load and bear the responsibility. It is not "your church," nor "my church," but "our church." All of us have a part in it.

II. MY DREAM CHURCH IS A LIVE CHURCH

The deadest thing in the world is a dead church; the greatest thing in the world is a live church. You can never hatch chickens in a Frigidaire, and souls are never born in a dead and cold church. Examine the records of our churches and you will find that those which are warm and alive have the largest numbers of converts every year. Christianity is a thing of life, and the church ought to be a thing of life. A dead business is a failing business; a dead church is a failing church.

On a hot, sultry night a group of people sat together talking about the hot weather. They just could not find any relief from the heat. Finally one of them said, "Let's go to prayer meeting over at Blank Church." "Where did you get such an idea?" another one asked. He replied, "We can get cool there—that is the coldest place in town." We do not want to have such a reputation for our church; we want it to be known as a warm, wide-awake church.

The live church attracts people—especially young people. They are our hope for tomorrow. Our active leaders of today will soon be gone; if our church does not attract the young people and line them up in service, the church will soon go out of existence. I ride down the road and I pass a stadium of twenty thousand seating capacity. It is absolutely empty because nothing is going on there. A few miles farther down the road I find another stadium packed with people. They are there because something is going on. If our church is alive, if something is going on, if our members are working, then the crowds will be coming all the time. We may have a beautiful building, a fine choir, and all the trappings of religion, but if we do not have a live, interested, enthusiastic group of workers, the church will not impress the world.

A Chinese Christian said to a mission board: "We want men with red-hot hearts to tell us of the love of Christ." A noted financier once said, "A bank will never be successful until the president takes that bank to bed with him." Napoleon was enthusiastic and would win in two weeks a campaign which would usually take a year for someone else to win. A great preacher said, "I want to burn out for God." Phillips Brooks said, "Let us beware of the loss of enthusiasm." Fox said, "Christians ought to be so filled with enthusiasm that they will light up the country for miles around." I want my church to be a live church.

III. My Dream Church Is a Trained Church

Training is essential to success everywhere. Our country wants better trained soldiers today; they do not send a man into battle the day he puts on a uniform. He is sent to camp where he is trained physically and mentally for his task. It takes training to make a good soldier. It would be foolish to put a man in the cockpit of a plane on the day he joins the Air Corps, and say to him, "Go to it." No, there must be months and months of training before he is even allowed in the air. It takes training to make a good pilot. In the olden days a man was a farmer because he was reared on a farm. He did things just the way his father did, he obtained meager results, and life was hard for him. Today we have agricultural colleges all over the land where men go to be trained to become better farmers. These men get more out of the land and life is easier and better for them. It takes training to make a good farmer.

On New Year's Day the great football teams go to the various Bowls. Thousands of people see them play. For two hours the teams charge up and down the gridirons and finally one team out of every two teams emerges victorious. Did each coach simply hand his team uniforms on New Year's Day and send them out to play? No, he spent long hours training the team, and the team spent long hours practicing before it could play the game. I have witnessed several major operations. I have stood near the operating table when a life hung in the balance, and when the surgeon plied his skilled fingers to save a man. The operation was a marvelous success, but could this man perform an operation on the first day he entered medical school? No, he spent years of study and work and intensive training before he became a surgeon. It takes training to make a good doctor.

If the soldier, the pilot, the farmer, the football player, the surgeon need training, the Christian worker needs training too. His task is delicate and important. He must do a good job, for the results count for time and for eternity. He must train himself to do the best possible job for God. When God wants a man for a big task, He calls a man who is trained. When His people were slaves in Egypt, and He needed a leader, He called Moses, the best trained man of his day. When another emergency arose and He wanted a man to give the Gospel to the world, He chose Paul, the best trained man of his day.

You can cut wood with a dull axe, but you can cut much better if that axe is sharpened a bit. God can use any man who surrenders to Him, but He can use that man in a greater way if he trains for God's service. Our church offers this training to every member — training in Bible study, training in missions, training in service; and every member ought to spend at least several years in this training. Yes, I want my church to be a trained church.

IV. My Dream Church Is a Faithful Church

Faithfulness is another essential of success. If we are to be successful anywhere, we must have faithfulness. We cannot build a successful business without faithful workers; we cannot build a successful church without them, either. If we are as faithful to our church as we are to our business, we will never miss a service. I tell you there is something wrong with us if we can be counted on in our business and in our social life but cannot be counted on in our church life. If we join any organization and pledge our allegiance to it, we ought to be faithful to that organization — I want them to be able to count on me.

If all of us were faithful in attending our church, it would not hold the crowds. Every debt would be paid, and the Gospel would be sent to the ends of the earth. We would never lack for workers and witnesses. The world would soon see the difference. We could lead that world toward Christ. Blessed is the faithful man: he gives the pastor strength and encouragement; he makes the church a power in the community; he lifts the burdens and keeps the work going; he makes others see that there is something of real value in religion.

Here are two members of the same church. Let us compare their lives and influence. One goes to church regularly. He lives a faithful Christian life, and does his part as it ought to be done. The other man comes to church once every few months; his life is worldly and God has but a tiny place in his heart. A third man is groping in sin. He is looking up for help in the battle of life. Which of these men will influence him most? Of which one would he say, "I wish I could be like him?" You know the answer — you simply have no influence for Christ or good unless you are faithful.

Someone said to an old soldier who had been in the battle of Waterloo, "What did you see while the battle was going on?" "Nothing but smoke and dust," he answered. "Well, what did you do?" The old man cried out, "Do! Why I stood by my gun." Oh, Christian, whether you can see anything good or not, whether you see any progress or not, whatever anyone else does — you stand by your gun! Be a faithful Christian! Christ's commendation is only to the faithful Christian: "Well done, thou good and faithful servant." Yes, I want my church to be a faithful church.

V. MY DREAM CHURCH IS A TITHING CHURCH

If it is a Bible church it must be a tithing church. A recent newspaper article tells us how the Mohammedans put us to shame in the matter of giving. In 1945 their spiritual leader had an anniversary and they gave him his weight in diamonds. This made a gift of $25,000,000. On an anniversary some years ago they gave him twice his weight in gold. We are not asked to give to a human being. We are asked to give to Christ in order to bless the world.

We admire the missionary who gives up everything and goes to a faraway land to spread the Gospel. Yet we "squawk" when we are called on to give a dollar to missions. The least any Christian can do is to give a tenth of his income to God as taught by the Bible. Many Christians will not do this because they do not have enough faith in God. God says, "You look after My work, and I will look after you. You seek My kingdom first, and I will add all things unto you. You plow My ground, and I will bring forth your fruit."

Right here in our church I can show you two types of people. There are those who have learned the joy of tithing. God has sent rich blessings into their lives. But there are those who have cut their pledges, who have withheld God's money. Today they suffer as a consequence of their actions. You are not asked to tithe so that the church can get your money; you are asked to tithe so that God can have you. He wants the opportunity of using and blessing you, and of giving you the joy of a surrendered will. Yes, I want my church to be a tithing church.

VI. MY DREAM CHURCH IS A SOUL-WINNING CHURCH

If a church is not a soul-winning church, why does it exist? The church is the only organization in the world which has this aim as its sole purpose. If our church fails here, its work is in vain.

It was Christmas time; I was talking to one of our men who had been a church member just a few months. He told of the happiness and joy that had come to his heart since he lined up with Christ and the church. He said that life was altogether different and better and more blessed for him and for his family. This same happiness and peace and joy are sought today by many people, but they are seeking in the wrong direction. Oh, let's go and tell them about our Saviour and the joy they will find in following Him!

One of our missionaries to Africa tells about an old blind man who came groping his way to the hand-built hospital in the jungle. This old man was a poor, ragged, hungry beggar, and the missionary took him in and fed and clothed him. He told the old man that he could perform an operation on his eyes, and possibly give him his sight, but that he would be taking a great risk. The old man told him to go ahead, because he had nothing to lose. The operation was performed and on the day the bandages were removed, thank God, the old man could see. The missionary led this old man to Christ. One day the old man went back into the jungle and was gone for many months. On another day he came back to the hospital ·leading ten other blind men behind him. The missionary doctor took them in and was able to restore the sight of five of them. There are millions of people on this earth who are blind in sin. Thank God we can have a part in giving them their spiritual eyesight. I want my church to take its place by the side of Christ in ministering to the whole world and in bringing it to the foot of the Cross.

God help us to have a dream church for the glory of God. There is only one way to have it: all of us must give ourselves in faithful surrender to the work of Christ. Then, in that day when He comes for us, we will hear Him say, "Well done, thou good and faithful servant" (Matt. 25:21).

5

A Journey Through the Halls of Hell

But Abraham said, Son, remember that thou in thy life-
time receivedst thy good things, and likewise Lazarus evil
things; but now he is comforted, and thou art tormented
(Luke 16:25).

There are some journeys which I would like very much
to take. I would like to go again to the beautiful Hawaiian
Islands. I would like to take a trip to the cities of South
America. I would like to travel through Europe and the
Holy Land. But there is one journey which I never want
to take — a journey to hell. If one goes there, he never re-
turns. If one goes there, an eternity of suffering faces him.
But in imagination let us take that journey. Let us go down
the halls of hell and look in on a few people who are spend-
ing an eternity there. We would not think of going alone,
so let us ask the Angel Gabriel to escort us on the journey.

As we enter hell we hear the groans and cries of the helpless souls who passed God by in this world. Just remember
that not one of them had to come here. No man is forced
to go to hell; it is his own choice. A Saviour died upon a
cross to save men from all of this, but since they have rejected Him there is now no hope for them. Some were high
and mighty in the world; some were rich and proud. But
here they have no power, no authority, no hope.

I. "Am I My Brother's Keeper?"

As we go down the hall we hear a man screaming, "Am
I my brother's keeper?" We ask the angel who this man is
and he tells us that it is Cain, who slew his brother Abel.

53

Then we remember our Bible (Gen. 4:1-12). Adam and Eve had two sons, Cain and Abel. They were taught to worship God. They were taught how to bring their offerings to the Lord. The day came when both sons came to the altar. Abel killed a lamb and offered it upon the altar. As the smoke ascended, God accepted this blood offering which was offered in faith by Abel. But Cain was wicked and proud. He brought the fruit which he had raised and offered it. God turned the offering down, and Cain became very angry. He went out into the field, found his brother, slew him and buried him. God then came down and spoke to Cain, "Where is Abel thy brother?" And Cain answered, "Am I my brother's keeper?" "I know what you have done," said God. "His blood cries out to me from the ground." And God pronounced a curse upon Cain.

Why is Cain in hell? Is it because he was a murderer? No, many murderers have repented and found grace in the sight of God. Cain is there because he would not come through God's way of salvation. All through the Bible salvation had to come through sacrifice and blood. Hebrews 9:22: "Without shedding of blood is no remission." As a supreme sacrifice, the Son of God poured out His rich, red, royal blood for the salvation of all men. The way to escape hell is to come through the bloodstained way to God. Cain was too proud to take this way.

Today men are trying to find salvation in the wrong way. Many pulpits refuse to preach a Gospel of blood. They call it "inelegant"; they talk of a "slaughterhouse religion." But this is God's way, the only way of salvation. The Gospel is good news, but when you take the blood out of the Gospel you have cut the heart out. The good news is gone, no life is left, and there is no hope for the soul. Let us not follow the false religions of the world, but let us come God's way, the blood-sprinkled way, the way of the Cross.

I must needs go home by the way of the cross,
There's no other way but this.
I shall ne'er get sight of the Gates of Light,
If the way of the cross I miss.

Now Cain went to hell because he rejected God's way. But someone says: "There ought to be more ways than one to be saved. If I live a good life and give to charity and pay my debts, I ought to go to heaven." But if God sets up a plan, there can be no other way. We accept man's imperatives, why not accept those of God? Two plus two equals four — we accept that. There are thirty-six inches in a yard and one hundred cents in a dollar. We do not argue with these standards. Why should we argue with the standards God has set up? He has one way of salvation. We are to come by repentance and faith to the blood-stained Cross, where we accept His Son as our Saviour. This is the only way to be saved.

Now Cain could have repented and could have gone to heaven. He could have said to God, "I am wrong and I see that you are right. I do now come unto Thee in faith and ask Thee to forgive me and save me." But he refused to do this, so we hear him crying out in hell, "Am I my brother's keeper?"

II. "Let Us In! Let Us In!"

We go down the hall and we hear a large group crying, "Let us in! Let us in!" The angel tells us that those are the people who lived in Noah's day.

Then we remember our Bible again (Gen. 6-8). The people of Noah's day were wicked and sinful. God decided to destroy them. But He found one righteous man, Noah. He told Noah to build an ark and to bring his family and certain animals into the ark; then God would destroy the earth with a flood. Noah began to build, giving part of his time to building, and part of his time to preaching. We can imagine that he worked on the ark by day and preached by night. He told the people that judgment was coming, that there would be a day of reckoning and that God would destroy the world with a flood. They laughed at him, saying, "You old fool. Who ever heard of such a thing?"

Noah preached for 120 years, but the people kept on sinning, while Noah kept on building the ark. One day God said, "Come in, Noah, the flood is coming." Noah and his family and the animals which God had selected went into the ark and God shut the door. Then the windows of heaven opened up, the rain began to fall, the fountains of the deep opened up and the water gushed out. The water rose higher and higher. The scoffers changed their tune; they ran to the ark, beat upon the door and cried out, "Let us in, Noah, you were right and we were wrong, let us in." But Noah said, "I am sorry, God has shut the door and I can't open it. I warned you for 120 years and now it is too late for repentance."

These people sinned away their days of grace and opportunity. Today the true preacher preaches like Noah. He declares that God has prepared an ark, even Jesus Christ, that judgment is coming, and he urges people to come in before it is too late. But what are so many people doing today? They are scoffing at the idea of a judgment; they are forgetting that they must face God; they are laughing at Bible truth. They are forgetting that "it is appointed unto man once to die and after this the judgment."

Sometime ago I sat in a group of 150 business men. I knew that only a few of them were real Christians. The others were giving their time and thought to business, to social life, to sports and the things of this life only. I said to myself, "This is a picture of the world today. I preach to men; I try to warn them. A few of them come to Christ, but the majority of them are going on down the pathway of life, leaving Christ out and forgetting the day of judgment."

Oh, friend, the door is open now, but some day it will be

shut. You will be lost forever. Now the men of Noah's day could have repented. Suppose after 119 years they had said, "Noah, you are right. We know that there is a God and that we are lost sinners, but we have come now to turn from our sins and to put our faith in God." We know God well enough to know that He would have held back the flood. But they would not repent, so they must spend eternity in hell, crying out, "Let us in! Let us in!"

III. A Woman Weeping and Painting Her Face

Down the hall we find a woman weeping and painting her face. The angel tells us that this is Jezebel, and we remember her well (I Kings 21; II Kings 9).

Jezebel was one of the most wicked women who ever lived. She was queen of Israel. Her husband Ahab wanted a certain vineyard which belonged to a godly man by the name of Naboth. Naboth would not sell the vineyard, so Jezebel said to Ahab, "I'll get that vineyard for you." She had Naboth brought to trial and paid evil men to testify against him. Then they took poor Naboth out and stoned him to death. Jezebel came back to her husband, saying, "Ahab, you can have your vineyard now. Naboth is dead."

But God will not let such sin go unnoticed. He sent a message to Elijah, "Go and tell that woman that one of these days the dogs will lick her blood and eat her flesh." But the years went by and nothing happened. Jezebel must have said, "I am a smart woman; I was able to get by with my sin." But she couldn't get by with sin, and neither can you and I.

One day Jehu came riding toward the palace. Jezebel wanted to gain favor with him. She painted her face and looked out the window as he approached. Jehu cried out: "Who is for us?" When two eunuchs appeared at the window Jehu said to them, "Throw her down." They threw Jezebel down upon the pavement and Jehu drove his horses and heavy chariot over her prostrate body. Later he said to his servants: "She is a king's daughter; go and bury her." But when they went to look for her body, they could find only a few bones remaining. The dogs had licked her blood and eaten her flesh as God had said they would.

You cannot fight God and get away with it. You can't say, "My sin will never catch up with me." There is Jezebel in hell, painting her face in screaming agony. She could have repented; she could have come to God; she could have confessed her sin and God would have saved her and taken her to heaven; but she would not repent, so she suffers in hell forever.

IV. A Man and Woman Running From Something

As we walk down the halls of hell we see a man and woman running from something. The angel tells us that the man is Herod and the woman is Herodias (Mark 6:14-29). Herod went to Rome, took his brother's wife, brought her back to Jerusalem and lived with her. One day a preacher named John confronted Herod. Listen to that brave preacher as he says to the king: "You are living in sin. You can't take another man's wife and get by with it." This made Herodias angry and she forced Herod to put John the Baptist in prison.

When the king's birthday came around, Herodias was still angry. She said, "I will get even with that preacher, if it is the last thing I ever do." So she said to her daughter, "Go and dance for the king and try to please him. He will soon be drunk and will give you anything that you ask of him. When he makes this offer, tell him that you want the head of John the Baptist on a charger. I'll show that preacher that he can't talk to me like that and get away with it." The daughter goes in to dance before the king, and soon the king is offering her a choice of anything that she desires. She asks for the head of John the Baptist. Herod knows that he has done the wrong thing, but he has to stand by his word or lose face with his courtiers. He has John beheaded and sends the head in to Herodias on a charger.

When the preacher's head was brought to Herodias, we can imagine that she looked upon it and said, "You'll never bother me any more; I have shut your mouth forever. You are through." But a few weeks later she and Herod were eating dinner. A servant burst in, crying out, "A great prophet has arisen and is performing some mighty miracles. The whole country is going after him." The king leaped to his feet and cried out, "That is John the Baptist; he has risen from the dead." But it wasn't John, it was Jesus.

Herod, your conscience is troubling you, isn't it? You are not able to sleep, are you? You cut off the preacher's head and his blood is upon your hands. Now you are going to pay for it, for "whatsoever a man soweth, that shall he also reap" (Gal. 6:7). So we can imagine that down in hell Herod and Herodias always think that the head of John the Baptist is chasing them. The head is not there; they just cannot escape their conscience. Memory in hell is an awful thing.

Now these two people could have repented. They could have gone out to Jesus. They could have fallen at His feet saying, "We are sinners; we are living in sin; we killed John the Baptist. But we are now repenting and we are going to straighten out our sordid lives. Is there any mercy for us? Is there any forgiveness for us?" Right then Jesus would have forgiven them and saved them. But they didn't come to Him; they didn't repent. They lived and died in their sin, and they died and went down to hell.

Your sin is not as great as theirs. You have never killed anyone; you have lived a pretty decent life. But if you don't repent of your sins and trust Jesus according to the Bible, you will surely go down to hell and suffer there with Herod and Herodias.

V. A Man Washing His Hands

We go down the halls of hell and see a man washing his hands. He screams in agony. A woman by his side keeps on saying: "I told you not to do it! I told you not to do it!" The angel tells me that this man is Pilate and the woman is his wife (Matt. 27:11-26).

One day Jesus stood before Pilate, the governor at that time. He knew that Jesus was a different man. He knew that He was a good man, for he said, "I can find no fault in Him." Pilate should have released Him, but the mob cried, "Crucify Him!" Now Pilate was a politician, and he wanted to gain favor with the people. So he stifled his own conscience and turned Christ over to be crucified.

Since Pilate's time, many men have preferred the favor of the crowd to the salvation of Christ. The crowd says: "Come and drink with us, come and go our way, drown your conscience and let's have a good time. Come on and go along with us." And some poor deluded fellow stifles his conscience because he wants to be popular with the crowd. He goes off into worldliness and sin; God is left out; and at last he ends up in hell.

Our young people are having a fierce and bitter fight during high school and college life. This fight extends out into business and social life. They have been taught that certain things are wrong. Other students do not believe this, so they put the pressure on our young people, telling them that they must do this and that, so that they will not become wet blankets. The temptation is strong and many boys and girls fall, but I tell you that it does not pay, here or hereafter. May God give them the grace to stand up for the right. Pilate fell and he has been washing his hands in hell ever since.

But Pilate was warned. There was a time when he wavered, not knowing whether to condemn Jesus or release Him. As he stood there he felt a tug at his sleeve. He looked around and found his wife there. "Honey," she said, "don't do anything against this man. I have been told in a dream that it would be tragic for you to oppose Him." Pilate's conscience cried out also: "Look out, Pilate, you are about to do something which will damn your soul forever. You can't trifle with Jesus, the Son of the Living God. He is the Saviour of the world and the dearest Beloved of the Father's heart. Look out, Pilate." But Pilate went ahead, condemned Christ and finally found his way down to hell.

Pilate was not the only one. You have been confronted with a choice. Your conscience has told you to leave your sin and follow Jesus. You have been warned time after time, but you go on in sin. One day you will join Pilate in hell, and all through eternity you will be sorry that you did not listen.

Pilate could have gone to heaven. After the crucifixion, after the resurrection, he could have fallen at the feet of Jesus and said, "I am sorry, Lord, I do believe in You now. Forgive me and save me." And Jesus would have done it, for He promises that He will in no wise cast out any who come to Him. But he didn't come to Jesus, so we leave him washing his hands in hell.

VI. "I Have Betrayed Innocent Blood"

We go down the hall and hear a man crying, "I have betrayed innocent blood." The angel tells us: "This is Judas, who betrayed Christ." (See Matt. 26:14-16; 47-50; 27:3-10.)

Christ selected this man to be His disciple. Judas walked with Him over three years. He heard His wonderful teachings; he saw His marvelous miracles; he served as treasurer of the group. But he wound up in hell, because his heart was not right. There is a great lesson here. You can go to church faithfully and serve well and give generously, and still be lost. You are lost because your heart is not right with God. Simply making a confession and being baptized and joining a church does not make the heart right. There must be an inner change: you must be born again.

By the way that some people live and act and talk, you know that they have not had an experience with Jesus. When you've had that, you become a different person. When I see church members who have such a little spirit about everything, I know that they have not caught the spirit of Jesus. If they are stingy and critical and faultfinding and worldly, I know they are not like Jesus; I know that they do not belong to Him.

Here is another lesson from Judas. He loved money so much that he sold his soul for it. The enemies of Christ promised him thirty pieces of silver to betray Christ. Judas agreed, saying, "I know where he prays and when He comes from the place of prayer, I will kiss Him and you will know that He is the Christ." The plot was carried out and Judas received the money. But the money did not make him happy. Remorse overtook him. He said, "I have betrayed innocent blood. Let us rue the bargain." But they laughed him to scorn and he went out and hanged himself.

Some people say, "I am going to get money; nothing else matters." They sell their souls to get it, but it carries them down to hell. The love of money has put many a man in hell.

But Judas could have repented. If he had done so, Jesus would have forgiven him. But he didn't do so, therefore we must leave him in hell, where he continually cries, "I have betrayed innocent blood."

VII. "BROTHER, BROTHER"

We go down the hall and hear a man screaming, "Brother, brother!" The angel says this is the rich man that Jesus told about. He lived sumptuously, but he left God out, and even permitted Lazarus to starve at his gate (Luke 16:19-31).

But why is he crying, "Brother"? When he first reached hell he looked up into Paradise and saw Abraham there, with Lazarus in his bosom. When he cried out for a drink of water, Abraham said unto him, "Between us and you there is a great gulf fixed. We cannot come to you and you cannot come to us." Then the man, realizing that there was no help for him, thought of his five brothers. "I have five brothers at home," he said; "send Lazarus to them, that he might warn them to repent, so that they will not come to this place." But Abraham said, "They have the law and the prophets. If they won't hear them, they won't hear one who arose from the dead."

We see here that the people in hell are interested in the people on earth. They know what hell is; they know the awful agony of it; and they don't want anyone to come there. If they could speak to you today, they would warn you to repent of your sins and to come to Jesus in order that you might be spared. Today we have an open Bible, and the Gospel is plainly preached, but men will not repent. Even if one came back from the dead, these sinners would say, "Well, you may have something there, but I love my sin and I will hold on to it a little longer."

The rich man could have been saved. Wealth will not keep you out of heaven, unless you make it your god. But he didn't repent, so he died and went to hell. We hear him crying out, "I am tormented in these flames."

VIII. "Almost, Almost"

Down the hall we hear a man screaming, "Almost, almost!" Gabriel tells us: "This is King Agrippa, but he is not a king now. He is just a poor lost soul suffering forever in hell." (See Acts 26.)

One day Agrippa heard a sermon by the greatest preacher in the world, the Apostle Paul. At the end of the sermon Agrippa was trembling all over. Paul said to him, "You know the prophets; you have read the Book. God has spoken to your soul; the Spirit has moved upon your heart. I wish that you would act upon the truth and give your heart to Christ." But Agrippa only said, "Almost thou persuadest me to be a Christian." It is not enough to hear the Gospel and to feel the power of the Spirit. You must act, you must surrender, you must give your heart to Christ.

What is the most tragic thing in the world? It is simply to go through life, to hear the Gospel, to come almost to Christ, then to go on without Him and to wind up in hell. In hell Agrippa remembers that he came within an inch of salvation — he was almost persuaded. But he shook off the feeling and went out to be lost forever. I have seen scores of people in the church who listened attentively and who knew that God was speaking to their hearts. They shook like a leaf in the autumn wind; their eyes were filled with tears. Almost they surrendered, almost they stepped out, almost they gave their hearts to Jesus. But they shook off that feeling and went back out into a busy world, forgot all about it and went down to their doom.

Now, Agrippa could have repented. He could have called Paul out of prison and said, "Paul, you stirred my soul the other day. I know I am lost and Christ alone can save me. I want to give my heart to Him now." And Christ would have saved him right then.

You, too, have been almost persuaded. You have been saying, "Someday I will make things right with God. I will give my heart to Christ. I will follow Him and be His child." But there is a great danger in saying, "Someday." Satan will lead you to put the matter off again and again. Then one day when death slips up to summon you, it will be too late for repentance. Oh, come to Jesus now!

General William Booth tells a story of a family which lived in London. There were four in this family, the mother and the father, and a son and a daughter. They were avowed enemies of the Gospel of Christ. They were so antagonistic that they declared they never wanted a Christian to enter their home. In the community there was a young Salvation Army girl who yearned and prayed for their salvation. When she heard that the son was sick, she decided to go and visit them in spite of their opposition. She climbed the stairs and paused for breath just outside the apartment door. Then she heard the voice of the father as he said, "Hold on, son, hold on. You may die but there is nothing beyond. We have read all the books; we have reasoned it all out; we know there is nothing beyond. Soon you will drift off into peaceful sleep and that will be all. Hold on, son."

Then the girl heard the sobbing cry of the mother, "My precious boy, it breaks my heart to see you go. But don't be afraid. We have investigated all the possibilities of the future life and there is nothing out there. You will soon be asleep. Hold on, son, hold on."

Then she heard the sister say, "Don't falter now, brother. You know that we decided long ago that there is nothing beyond. Soon you will go to sleep and that will be all. Just hold on."

Then she heard the voice of the boy, laden with despair and grief, "That's all right," he said, "but there is nothing for me to hold on to. I am going into the dark and there is nothing for me to hold on to."

Oh, friend without Christ, if you have not placed your hand in the nail-scarred hand of Jesus, there will be nothing for you to hold on to in the hour of death. You will simply sink into hell. But Jesus stretches out His hand to you today. He loves you; He wants to save you. He invites you to come and find peace and joy and eternal life in Him. Don't go to hell. Come to Jesus today and get on the road to heaven.

6

Since Jesus Came Into My Heart

For we ourselves also were sometimes foolish, disobedient, deceived, serving divers lusts and pleasures, living in malice and envy, hateful, and hating one another. But after that the kindness and love of God our Saviour toward man appeared, not by works of righteousness which we have done, but according to his mercy he saved us, by the washing of regeneration, and renewing of the Holy Ghost; which he shed on us abundantly through Jesus Christ our Saviour; that being justified by his grace, we should be made heirs according to the hope of eternal life. This is a faithful saying, and these things I will that thou affirm constantly, that they which have believed in God might be careful to maintain good works. These things are good and profitable unto men (Titus 3:3-8).

Some years ago Dr. Jacob Gartenhaus preached one Sunday night in a church in Shawnee, Oklahoma. He was told that an Austrian Jew was attending the Oklahoma Baptist University, which is located at Shawnee. On Monday morning Dr. Gartenhaus walked through the snow to visit this man in his dormitory room. The reception which he received from the student was colder than the weather. This young man accused Dr. Gartenhaus of betraying the Jewish people. Of course Dr. Gartenhaus told him that he was doing the best thing possible for the Jews by pointing them to the Saviour who could end all of their sufferings. He then left some tracts with the student, knowing that as soon as he left the room they would be thrown into the wastebasket. A few years later Dr. Gartenhaus was back in Shawnee for a Sunday night service. The pastor called on a young man to come forward and lead the evening prayer. Dr. Gartenhaus was greatly surprised when the young Jewish student, whom he had talked to on that Monday morning, came forward and led a fervent prayer. In the army this young man had been won to Christ by some ardent Christians. A wonderful change had been wrought in his life by the Lord Jesus Christ.

My text tells about another young Jew, whose name was Saul. He had gone his way as "the chief of sinners." But one day on the Damascus Road he met Jesus and now the man who had fought Christ became His most lovable and loyal follower. Our story is the same: Jesus makes the difference. There has been a wonderful change in our lives since Jesus came into our hearts.

As we look at these verses in the Book of Titus, we see five things. We see our Past, our Portion, our Position, our Participation and our Profit.

I. Our Past

For we ourselves also were sometimes foolish, disobedient, deceived, serving divers lusts and pleasures, living in malice and envy, hateful, and hating one another (v. 3).

This verse tells us what we used to be, before Jesus came into our hearts. You will note that we have been guilty of three kinds of sin.

1. *First, we were disobedient toward God.* We knew how God wanted us to live; we knew His commandments; we knew His laws and teachings. But we disregarded these things; we disobeyed God; we cast His laws aside. All sin first of all is against God. If we get right with Him sin will have no dominion over us. Jesus had no sin, because His heart was right toward God.

When we get right with God, the sin question is settled. I am thinking now of a certain home which was going on the rocks. The husband and wife were drinking and quarreling and absolutely leaving God out of their lives. Saturday night was spent in worldly indulgences, so they had no time for the Lord on Sunday. The wife called me to come to see them one night. I talked and prayed with them and the next Sunday they started to church. In a little while they were actively serving the Lord. They gave up the things of the world; all their troubles were ironed out; and they found a great happiness. There is no trouble in a home which Christ cannot cure.

Dr. Charles E. Fuller, of the Old Fashioned Revival Hour, was making a trip on a plane. When he gave his name to the stewardess, a young lady in the seat next to him overheard his conversation. She asked him if he were the Dr. Fuller who preached on the radio and he told her that he was. She then said to him, "I have been waiting to see you and thank you for what you did for our home. My husband was a fine man, but he was drinking very heavily. For years I had prayed for his salvation. One Sunday morning he happened to be sober. He sat down by the radio and heard your broadcast. When you finished your message he fell on his knees by the radio and gave his heart to Christ. He later joined the church and since that time our home has been a little bit of heaven on earth." Yes, when you get right with God, life straightens out. But in the past we were guilty of disobedience to God.

2. *Next, we were guilty of the sins of the flesh.* "Divers lusts and pleasures." These sins of the flesh are those which satisfy the fleshly nature. They are adultery, drinking, cheating, gambling, lust for money, and other like sins. These are the sins that you can see, the sins that you can put your finger on. Today America is crushed down with these sins. Our country is filled with liquor stores. We spend eleven billion dollars per year on intoxicants. Thousands of girls and boys under eighteen are arrested each year.

These are the sins which have ruined many nations in the past. Babylon and Rome and Egypt were all wealthy and powerful, but these lustful sins crept in and these nations went down to ruin. This will be true of any nation and any individual. In the past we were guilty of sins of the flesh.

3. *Next, we were guilty of the sins of the disposition.* "Living in malice and envy, hateful and hating one another." These are the sins committed by so many church members. The insidious thing about these sins is that you cannot put your finger on them. Some people in our churches would not dare to give way to the flesh in a sin which would hurt only one or two people, but they indulge in these sins which hurt hundreds. They would not dare to gamble or cheat or go to a picture show, but they think nothing of hating people, of malicious gossip and of hurting others. Oh, that Christians would be Christlike and have the spirit which makes them love one another. Maybe you have not been guilty of a fleshly sin; but if you have envy, malice and hatred in your heart you are just as guilty, before God, as an adulterer or gambler.

Now the apostle says that these are the things of the past — disobedience toward God and indulgence in the sins of the flesh and of the disposition. These sins were put away in his life. Have you put them away?

II. OUR PORTION

But after that the kindness and love of God our Saviour toward man appeared, not by works of righteousness which we have done, but according to his mercy he saved us, by the washing of regeneration, and renewing of the Holy Ghost; which he shed on us abundantly through Jesus Christ our Saviour (vv. 4-6).

1. *The first thing in our portion is that Christ loved us.* Look at the contrast here. On our part we were disobedient toward God and indulged in the sins of the flesh and the disposition. On God's part He was loving us. He loved us while we were sinners, while we were rebelling against Him.

Here is a man who has an only son. All of his hopes are wrapped up in that boy. One day a wicked criminal kills this son in cold blood. The father is brokenhearted. The sun goes out of his sky and the stars out of his life. Does the father say to the murderer, "God bless you, sir, you killed my son, but I love you and will do anything for you." He would be a very unusual father if he felt that way. But God felt that way, for He is an unusual Father. He had an only Son and you and I murdered Him. Our sin created the Cross. Our sin nailed Him to the tree. Our sin pressed the thorns upon His brow and thrust the spear into His side. We killed the Only-begotten Son of God. But how does God feel about it? He loves us and says that He will do anything in the world for us and finally take us to heaven. Oh, who can measure the heighth and depth of the love of our God!

2. *The second thing in our portion is that He saved us.* This text plainly tells us that we are not saved by the good things that we have done, but because of His mercy. Our salvation comes to us not through joining a church or giving money or performing good deeds, but because of the mercy and grace of God. A man looks at himself and sees only a poor lost sinner. But he looks at One hanging on the Old Rugged Cross and he finds hope for his soul.

> Mercy there was great, and grace was free,
> Pardon there was multiplied to me;
> There my burdened soul found liberty,
> At Calvary.

3. *The third part of our portion is that He gave us the Holy Spirit.* When a child is born into a home he is not left to walk alone, but is given a mother to care for him. This mother helps him, comforts him, and teaches him to face life. Likewise, when a soul is born into the kingdom of God the Lord says, "I will not cause you to walk alone; I will send my Holy Spirit to walk with you." He will care for you, comfort you and teach you to face the hard things of life. Thank God, we are not alone.

In the olden days the American Indians trained their boys in courage. Among other tests they would force the boy to spend a night in the forests among the wild animals. Of course, the boy would feel very lonely and afraid, but in the morning he saw his father standing behind the tree with arrow drawn, ready to protect his son. The boy didn't know it, but the father had been there all through the night. We are in a world of terror and strife, but we are not alone. God the Holy Spirit is with us every hour, whether it be bright or dark. "Though I walk through the valley of the shadow of death, I will fear no evil: for thou art with me" (Ps. 23:4). Yes, this is our portion. God loved us and saved us and gave us the Holy Spirit.

III. Our Position

That being justified by his grace, we should be made heirs according to the hope of eternal life (v. 7).

We are the heirs of God. When Henry Ford died he left millions to his heirs. But God has greater wealth than that waiting for us. Some years ago Mrs. McLean died in Washington. She was the owner of the famous Hope diamond. In her will she specified that this diamond was not to be given to her daughter until twenty years had passed by. But it is not that way with our Heavenly Father. We don't have to wait for the good things He has for us. We begin to receive them just as soon as we trust Christ as our Saviour.

If we are the heirs of God, we have a high position and we ought to live up to it. There are some things which a king's son cannot do; there are some places to which he must never go. There are also some things which God's child cannot do and some places which he can never enter. Every believer ought to say, "I am a Christian, a child of God, therefore I must live up to my high position."

A missionary was preaching in India. At the most interesting part of his sermon a woman left the building, stayed away several minutes, and then returned. After the service she told the missionary why she had left. She said, "I was so interested in what you were saying that I wondered whether or not you lived out these teachings in your everyday life. I went out and asked your carriage driver about it. He said that you lived just as you talked, therefore I was glad to come back and listen to you again." Yes, the missionary remembered his position and lived up to it. The world will never listen to us unless we live up to our high position.

You and I have an exalted position: we are the children of God. We are not to gloat over it, but we are to rejoice in it and live up to it.

IV. Our Participation

This is a faithful saying, and these things I will that thou affirm constantly, that they which have believed in God might be careful to maintain good works (v. 8a).

What is Paul saying here? He is simply saying that after we become Christians we should be careful to maintain good works. There are some who start out well and they serve enthusiastically for a while, but they do not maintain their good works.

Sometime ago I had lunch with my oldest brother. He pointed out a man at another table and told me that this man was a very active church member and that he taught a large class of men in a certain church. In a few minutes this man finished his meal and came by our table. My brother introduced me to him. I said to the man, "I am glad to know that you are active in your church and that you teach a Sunday school class." He dropped his head a bit and then said, "Well, I am not in that church any longer. I didn't like something the pastor did so I took my membership out of that church." I asked him if he had joined another church and he told me that he had not done so. His church letter was at home. He began in a good way; he was working for the Lord; but he was not careful to maintain good works. Our churches are filled with people like that. What a mighty force they could be for the cause of Christ if they faithfully served Him, regardless of everything else under the sun.

General William Booth and Rudyard Kipling were to sail on the same ship. As they stood on the deck of the ship talking to each other, General Booth saw a group of Salvation Army people conducting a street service nearby. He excused himself, went down to the group and joined in the service. He spoke of Christ to the crowds and later came back to join Mr. Kipling. "General Booth," said Mr. Kipling, "you made a ludicrous sight down there, playing the tambourine and with your cape blowing in the wind." And General Booth replied, "Mr. Kipling, if I can keep people out of hell by standing on my head and playing the tambourine with my toes, I will learn to do it." He believed in maintaining good works. We are saved for heaven but also for earth. We are saved to sing in glory but we are also saved to serve down here. If we have been saved, we ought to be busy for the Lord.

V. Our Profit

These things are good and profitable unto men (v. 8b).

Does it pay a man to leave the Devil's service and line up on God's side and serve Him? It certainly does. It pays for time and eternity. Every man who has tried it has found that it does pay. It pays right here in this world. If there were no afterlife, no heaven and no hell, it would still pay a thousand ways to be a Christian here. But there is more to it. It pays through a long eternity. Surely it is "all this and heaven, too."

Dr. Jesse Hendley was pastor of a church in Atlanta. A good woman in his church lost her only son during the war. Dr. and Mrs. Hendley went out to see this brokenhearted mother. They talked and prayed together. As Mrs. Hendley put her arms around the woman, the woman broke out into a paroxysm of grief. But soon she straightened up and said, "The last time my boy had a furlough he planned a surprise for me. I did not know that he was coming home until the door was flung open and I heard him say, 'Hello, Mom.' In a moment we were in each other's arms. He has gone on to heaven now and before long I will be going too. I know that when I step inside the gates I will hear a familiar voice. My boy will cry out, 'Hello, Mom,' and he will be in my arms again." Oh, yes, it does pay to trust Christ! It pays here and it pays hereafter.

A young Englishman from a fine family was blinded by an accident when he was ten years of age. Despite this handicap he won many honors in school, and as a young man he won the hand and heart of a lovely girl, although he could not see her face. A few weeks before the wedding day a famous surgeon performed an operation upon the boy's eyes. The day set to remove the bandages turned out to be the day of the wedding. The young man came into the church with his father and stood there waiting for his bride. Soon the bride stood before him. The surgeon stepped up behind the boy and began to remove the bandages. It was a tense moment. But in a few minutes the last bandage was removed. The young man was able to see and the first face that he saw was the face of the girl who loved him, even though he was blind. He gazed for a long time into her eyes, then took her in his arms and said, "At last, at last!"

Someday life's battles will be over for us. The blindness of earth will be removed. At last, at last we will be at Home. In that Home we will see Jesus and the ones that we have loved and lost. Then we will know that it was worth all the struggle of life, for God will be paying us off throughout all of eternity.

7

It Is No Secret

> For the king knoweth of these things, before whom also I speak freely: for I am persuaded that none of these things are hidden from him; for this thing was not done in a corner (Acts 26:26).

Several years ago Evangelist Billy Graham held a meeting in Los Angeles. In this meeting a radio singer named Stuart Hamblen was gloriously and wondrously converted. He turned away from his sinful and worldly ways, and since that time he has been going about the country, giving his testimony as to the saving grace and power of Jesus Christ. Out of his experience he wrote a song entitled: "It Is No Secret."

In this song he says:

It is no secret what God can do,
What He's done for others, He can do for you.
With arms wide open, He'll pardon you,
It is no secret what God can do.

But many centuries ago the Apostle Paul said the same thing in different words. Standing before King Agrippa he made a passionate appeal and preached a mighty sermon. He told of his own life and how he had lived against Christ; he told how he had been gloriously saved by the risen Saviour and how he was now going about preaching the Gospel. Then he said: "The king knows about these things. They were not done in a corner." He was simply saying that God has been doing some wonderful things, that there is no secret about it, that all these things have been revealed to men.

Where do you and I learn about these things? Where can we find the revelation of what God has done? We will not find the highest revelation in the world of nature, although God is revealed there. His footprint is on every mountain and stream and ocean. His handiwork is seen in the sun, the moon, the stars and the Milky Way. His touch is seen in every tree and flower and blade of grass. But the highest revelation of God's great works is found in the Book that He wrote — the Bible. These things are revealed to us by the Holy Spirit as we read the Bible. And what are the greatest things revealed in the Bible? They are the things concerning Christ. He is the center of the Bible, the subject of the Bible. He is the One who walks down every page and leaps out from every paragraph.

I. His Virgin Birth Was No Secret

Of all those who prophesied about Jesus in the Old Testament, surely Isaiah was the greatest. He told how Jesus would be born, how He would live and how He would die. Listen to Isaiah 7:14: "Therefore the Lord himself shall give you a sign; Behold, a virgin shall conceive, and bear a son, and shall call his name Immanuel."

God had made man in His own image and placed him in the world. But man sinned; he broke the laws of God; therefore he became subject to the penalty of a broken law. But God loved him and wanted to save him from this penalty. So God made His plans. His own Son would come down into the world and shed His blood for the sins of man. But how shall He get into the world? Shall He come down as a full-grown man and launch out upon His career? No, God chose that He should come as a little babe. He would grow up in the natural way, so that He would know all the sorrows and cares and temptations which come to man. He needed to know these things in order to fully sympathize with us in our woes.

So the prophecy of the Virgin Birth was given. Then seven hundred years pass slowly by. The great hour arrives:

the clock of eternity chimes out; it is time for the Saviour to be born. Now we see God picking out a human mother to bring His Son into the world. In Galilee He found a young woman named Mary who was engaged to Joseph. This young woman He selected to be the human mother of His divine Son. She was not to be worshiped; she was not to be a mediator between God and man; she was to be simply a human instrument who would bring God's Son into the world.

Now God's angel comes down to tell Mary of the approaching birth. Of course, she was greatly puzzled, for she had had no physical relations with any man. But the angel told her that the Holy Spirit would speak the child into being. She could look months ahead and see what this meant of disgrace and humiliation. No one would understand her; everyone would think that she was immoral. But she bowed her head and said, "Behold the handmaid of the Lord; be it unto me according to thy word" (Luke 1:38).

God later told Joseph to go ahead and marry her. We are plainly told in the Bible that there were no marital relations until after Jesus was born. Man was not going to have anything to do with this birth. It was to be all of God. Then the time came when Joseph took Mary to Bethlehem. They spent the night in a barn and on that night, while the angels sang on the Judean hillsides, the Saviour of the world was born and laid in a manger.

Billions of people have been born but there has never been a birth like this. Every other birth came into being through the fusion of two human personalities. Jesus came through the work of God, who used Mary as His human instrument to get the Saviour into the world. Yes, we believe in the Virgin Birth of Jesus Christ. It is no secret.

II. His Wonderful Life Was No Secret

Adam, the first man, committed sin. From Adam right on down to the last man who will ever come into the world, every man sins. But standing high above all men is the God-Man, Christ Jesus. He never sinned. He never had a sinful thought; He never spoke a sinful word; He never committed a sinful deed. This is the great difference between Jesus and all other men. "All have sinned, and come short of the glory of God" (Rom. 3:23). But in Jesus there was no sin. This fact marks the difference between Christianity and all other religions. All founders of other religions were human beings, guilty of sin. The founder of Christianity is a sinless Saviour.

Somewhere in the world there is a tree called the Judas tree. It produces a beautiful flower of brilliant crimson. The bee is drawn to it to gather honey. But every bee which lights upon this flower imbibes a fatal poison and drops dead beneath the tree. But I tell you that there was nothing in this world beautiful enough and sweet enough to attract Jesus into sin.

On one occasion He said, "Satan hath nothing in me." How true this was. Satan reached up to grasp Him and to pull Him down, but Satan failed every time.

His life was not only sinless; it was serviceable. Many men are born simply to live for a little while and to die without making any contribution to the world. But Jesus contributed to every life that He touched. Because of Him the blind man was enabled to see. The crippled man was made to walk. The deaf could hear; the dead were brought back to life again. Some people just go about, but Jesus went about doing good.

The motto of every commercial enterprise today is "Service." Every business advertises the kind of service it gives to those who patronize it. But there is always a price on that service; we don't get something for nothing. But Jesus, who served man as no other man has ever done, gave His service without money and without price. We never see Him taking anything for it. It was an unselfish service.

Can you imagine Jesus coming into the world, sitting down

and drinking in all the blessings of God, and never doing anything? Can you imagine Him living a life of ease? But many people do live like that. They take all and give nothing. They enjoy all and do nothing. Oh, if you want to be like Jesus, you should promote yourself to the servant class.

Along with His sinless life of service, we also remember the sermons which He preached. He spoke as no man had ever spoken before. He knew God and revealed Him to man. He knew man and pointed him to God. It was said of a great musician that he brought God down to man. It was said of another musician that he lifted man up to God. In His sermons Jesus did both.

Some of His sermons have been published in the Book. There is no secret about them, every man can read them. These sermons have touched more hearts and changed more lives than any sermons ever preached. When all other sermons have been forgotten, men will remember the sermons of Jesus and be blessed by them. There is no secret about His life: it was the greatest life ever lived.

III. His Vicarious Death Was No Secret

His great and perfect life rebuked the men of His time. His service put them to shame. His claims that He was the Son of God incensed them to red-hot anger. So these men plotted His destruction. They could find Him guilty of no wrong, so they trumped up their charges against Him and finally gained a verdict. He was sentenced to die on the Cross. His death was no secret thing; it took place on the high hill of Calvary where all the world could see it. As His perfect Son died, God turned His back, the angels wept in sorrow and the sun refused to shine. The lonely Saviour took our sins in His own body; He drank the cup of sorrow down to its bitterest dregs, He bled His life away so that you and I might have eternal life. Let us thank God for that death. If it had not happened there would have been no hope for us. If He had not died, you and I would be dead in trespasses and sin. If He had not suffered on Calvary we would have suffered forever in hell.

Because of His death we have forgiveness for sin. Sin had us in its grip, but through His death that grip is broken and our sins are forgiven.

During the Civil War a young soldier was sentenced to die. His mother went to President Lincoln and pleaded for a pardon. Lincoln issued this pardon and the boy's life was spared. When a cabinet member escorted her from the President's Office, she said: "I knew it was a lie." "What are you talking about?" asked the cabinet member. And she said, "They told me that Mr. Lincoln was an ugly man, but I declare that he is the handsomest man that I ever saw." The Cross of Calvary is an ugly thing, a thing of shame and disgrace. But when you and I come to Calvary our sins are forgiven and we realize that the Cross is the most beautiful thing in all the world, for it was there that Christ died to make us whole.

Because of His death we have hope. What hope does a man have who never looks in faith toward the Cross? He may live a good life; he may do many good works; he may give his money in a princely sum; but if his hope is in these things, he is a man without hope.

A rich man took a preacher through his wonderful new home. The preacher looked upon the displays of wealth on every side. Finally the man took him up into a tower and pointing in every direction he said to the preacher, "All that you can see is mine." The preacher replied, "It is fine that you have all of this property in every direction, but," said he, as he pointed his finger up toward heaven, "what do you have in that direction?" Let me tell you that you have nothing up there if you have not appropriated by faith all that Jesus did for you on the Cross.

Two sets of nails held Jesus to the Cross, the nails in His hands and the nails in His feet. But spiritually there was something else which held Him there. Mind you, He could have come down from the Cross if He had so desired. But His great love for us held Him to that tree until He had suffered all the agonies of hell for us, that we might have everlasting life. From that Cross He sends out this message to all the world, "Look unto me, and be ye saved, all the ends of the earth" (Is. 45:22). His death was no secret. The message of the Cross has gone out to all the world. To reject that message is to die; to accept it is to live forever.

IV. His Victorious Resurrection Was No Secret

When He walked upon the earth, He foretold His resurrection. He said, "The Son of man must suffer many things . . . and be slain, and be raised the third day" (Luke 9:22). But no one believed it, not even His closest friends. Peter could say, "Thou art the Christ, the Son of the living God" (Matt. 16:16). But no one had ever risen from the dead and no one believed that Jesus would do it. But He did arise. After a busy and active life, after His agony on the Cross, He rested for a while in the grave. But in a little while He rose up from the tomb, leisurely laid aside His grave clothes, stepped out of the grave and came forth to live forever. There is our hope, there in a risen Saviour.

Heathen art expresses its hopelessness in the face of death. Some heathen artists portray death as a ship gone to pieces, some as a harp with broken strings, some as a flower crushed beneath a heavy foot, some as the sands of time all run down in the hourglass. But the Christian points to the empty tomb and says, "Death isn't all. There is One who conquered the grave. Because He lives, we also shall live."

Dr. Harry Rimmer was talking to a Moslem in Egypt. This man was a high official, a refined and cultured gentleman. Dr. Rimmer said, "We believe that God has revealed Himself in three ways." Said the Moslem, "We believe the same thing." Dr. Rimmer said, "He has revealed Himself to us in the works of creation." "We believe that, also," said the Moslem. Dr. Rimmer said, "He has revealed Himself to us in a Book, the Bible." The Moslem said, "He has revealed Himself to us in a book also, the Koran." Dr. Rimmer said, "He has revealed Himself to us in a man, Jesus Christ." The Moslem said, "He has revealed Himself to us in a man, Mohammed." Dr. Rimmer said, "We believe that Jesus died to save His followers." The Moslem said, "We believe that Mohammed died for the people." "But," said Dr. Rimmer, "we believe that Jesus substantiated His claims by rising from the dead." The Moslem could only sadly reply, "We have no information concerning our prophet after his death."

This is the reason that Jesus is supreme. He is the only One who conquered death and triumphed over the grave. His resurrection is no secret; the world knows about it. Every Sunday we celebrate it.

V. His Ascension Was No Secret

After His resurrection He spent forty days upon the earth. He was seen by many people. He walked and talked with His disciples. But the time came when He must return to heaven, there to share with His Father the glory He had before the world began. One day He went with the disciples out to Olivet. There He gave them a new task and promised to be with them through His Spirit to the end of the age. As the disciples stood around Him, suddenly a cloud came down out of heaven and enveloped Him. He seemed to lean back upon this cloud. Then they saw the cloud going up and up and up, with Jesus on its bosom. The heavens opened up and suddenly He was out of sight. Surely all the joy bells of heaven rang and all the angels sang a happy song. For the Son was home — man could harm Him no more. At last He was at home in the Father's house.

What has Jesus been doing up there all these years? We are told that He has been intereceding for us, praying for us.

It is good to have a godly person here to pray for us, but it is glorious to have Jesus to intercede in our behalf at the Father's throne. It takes a living, ascended, reigning Saviour to help us. The world is too strong for us. We will be defeated if we don't have Jesus on our side.

In the olden days a famous violinist gave a concert in a Western town. After the concert, a grey-haired pastor was seen talking to the violinist. The next day the town was flooded with handbills, saying, "Come to the First Baptist Church tonight and hear the famous violinist play on his five thousand dollar violin. No admission charges." That night the church was crowded with people. The violinist came out and played his first number. The people had never heard such wonderful music. They laughed a little and cried a little. They applauded at the end of the number. The violinist smiled and began to tighten the strings of his violin. Suddenly a string snapped and the man in a fit of anger lifted the violin over his head and brought it down upon the pulpit, shattering the violin to pieces. He then sat down. . . . The crowd was astounded, for this man had destroyed a five thousand dollar violin. But the pastor came to the pulpit and said, "Learn a lesson. The violin which the artist used to stir your souls was worth sixty-four cents. The five thousand dollar violin is behind the curtain and he will play it for you in a minute. Here is the lesson — a sixty-four cent violin in the master's hand can make music fit for God's symphony orchestra; a little life in the hands of Jesus the Master can lift men toward God."

You and I are mighty small. But as we surrender to this great Saviour we become vessels fit for God's service. Men will then see our good works and know that we are possessed by a Higher Power.

VI. His Glorious Return Is No Secret

When He ascended up to heaven the disciples stood by in open-mouthed amazement. Where had He gone? What would happen next? Then two figures from the realms of glory appeared and said unto them, "Ye men of Galilee, why stand ye gazing up into heaven? this same Jesus, which is taken up from you into heaven, shall so come in like manner as ye have seen him go into heaven" (Acts 1:11).

It is no secret that Jesus is coming back to earth again. For many years this has been a neglected truth. But it has a prominent place in the Bible, and all over the world this blessed hope is being preached today. He is coming in the air to gather up all of His saints, both the dead and the living. Then He is coming back to earth with His own and here He will reign for a thousand years before the endless ages begin. I do not know when He is coming, but time has flown by and Bible prophecies have been fulfilled. We are now ready for the next step in the great prophetic drama, as portrayed by Paul in Thessalonians. "For the Lord himself shall descend from heaven with a shout, with the voice of the archangel, and with the trump of God: and the dead in Christ shall rise first: then we which are alive and remain shall be caught up together with them in the clouds, to meet the Lord in the air: and so shall we ever be with the Lord" (I Thess. 4:16-17).

A woman said to a preacher friend, "Do you believe that Jesus is coming soon?" The preacher replied, "I do not know for sure, but I believe that He will come very soon." "That is what I am afraid of," said the woman. "But," said the preacher, "I thought you were a Christian. Why are you afraid of His coming?" "I am saved," said the woman, "but my husband is unsaved. I am afraid that Jesus will come soon and my husband will be left behind and I will never see him again." Friend, are you ready for His coming?

I have talked to you of this wonderful Saviour, of His Virgin Birth, of His Wonderful Life, of His Vicarious Death, of His Victorious Resurrection, of His Ascension, of His Glorious Return. Let me ask you a question: Is Jesus yours?

Are you following Him? Are you living at your best for Him.

A certain girl visited a friend in a small town and was saved in a revival meeting. She then went back to Philadelphia to her home. Her parents were wealthy society people. When she told them of her conversion, they were not at all pleased. But she lived in a new world, she spoke a new language, she sang a new song. One night at the dinner table, her father said, "Alice, we have heard nothing but religion from you since you came home. There has been too much of it and we are going to call a halt. Tomorrow morning at nine o'clock you must meet your mother and me in the living room and make your decision about this fanaticism. You must give up your religion or leave our house forever." . . . The girl spent most of the night in prayer. The next morning she packed her suitcase and went downstairs. She set the suitcase down in the hall, spoke to her mother and father and then went over to the piano in the living room. Sitting down she began to play and sing:

> Jesus, I my cross have taken,
> All to leave, and follow Thee;
> Destitute, despised, forsaken,
> Thou, from hence, my all shalt be.

Her father could not stand it any longer. He went over to his daughter and threw his arms around her and said: "If you love Christ like that, even enough to give up everything for Him, there must be something to Christianity. How could I have Him as my Saviour?" In a little while she had led her father to faith in Jesus Christ.

Yes, Christ means everything to some people. What does He mean to you?

8

The Glory of the Big Book

Search the scriptures; for in them ye think ye have eternal life: and they are they which testify of me (John 5:39).

When I was boy our family library was very small, but I always liked to read. I borrowed every book I could obtain. I enjoyed reading Horatio Alger, the Rover Boys and Tom Swift. One day I took one of these books to school with me and during the study period I placed this book within my geography book, which was the largest book I had. I held it up before me so that the teacher could easily see that I was studying my geography. However, I became too interested in the story. She came around the back of the room and caught me with the forbidden book. I will draw the curtain on what happened, but I assure you that I was more careful thereafter.

But there was another Book in our home which was larger than any book I had ever seen. It was the family Bible. In the middle of the Bible there was a family record which gave the important dates of our family history. At the back of the Bible there was a "gallery of Scripture illustrations." Often on Sunday afternoon I would get the big Book down on the floor and read the great stories that it contained. I looked at the pictures of the mighty men of old and followed with interest their deeds of greatness and bravery. I have long since forgotten the stories of Horatio Alger, the Rover Boys and Tom Swift, but the stories and truths which I learned from the Big Book will linger in my heart forever.

Dr. R. G. Lee says that "the Bible is beyond other books as the river is beyond a drop of water, as the sun is beyond the candle, and as the mountain is beyond a grain of sand. It is the fountain in which martyrs have cooled their faces, the pillow upon which the saints of all ages have rested their hearts; it breaks the fetters of the slave, takes the pain out of parting, takes the sting out of death, takes the gloom out of the grave and gives us a hope that is steadfast and sure."

Oh, the glory of the Big Book! What is that glory?

I. It Is Glorious Because It Abides Forever

"The grass withereth, the flower fadeth: but the word of our God shall stand for ever" (Is. 40:8).

A human being writes a book, puts it on sale and it soon becomes the best seller. A few thousand copies are sold and before long this book is forgotten and another takes its place. The Bible was written by God Himself. It is the best seller of every year and it is never forgotten. It remains always the one abiding Book.

Every effort to destroy the Big Book has failed. Voltaire said, "One hundred years from now the Bible and Christ will be forgotten." But here is the irony of it in his case: the very room in which he spoke these words is now used as a Bible storehouse. So has been every effort to destroy the Bible. The haters of the Bible pass off the scene of action but the Bible lives on.

At the western end of the Mediterranean Sea there is a great rock called Gibraltar. The waves of the centuries have been beating against the great rock, but it still stands. In like manner the waves of the centuries have been beating against the Big Book, but yet it is as impregnable as ever.

Nineteen hundred years ago Jesus stood in the mighty temple and preached the Word. Today the mighty temple is gone, but the Word abides. Paul walked into Athens, looked upon the Parthenon and the great buildings of the Acropolis. He walked up the Appian Way to Rome and saw there the Colosseum and the Forum. These are gone but the Book which had such a great part in his life abides forever. Yes, one of the glories of the Big Book is that it abides. It is the Book of every month and every year.

II. It Is Glorious Because It Is a Revelation from God

What do we mean by revelation? Well, here is a family in Florida. The son grows up and goes to California, three thousand miles away. Once a month his mother writes him a long letter. She reveals the things that are going on at home and the thoughts of her own heart. She tells of the sickness in the family, the death of a neighbor, the birth of a new baby and the wedding of friends. We call this a human revelation.

God wanted to send a message to His children, so in the olden days He breathed on certain men and inspired them to write the Bible. He revealed how the world was made and His own great thoughts were put into the Book. The Book tells of the life and death of the men of old and the story of the Babe who was born in Bethlehem. It tells of a man's sin and God's love and Christ's sacrifice. It tells of man's power of choice and his opportunity for salvation. It tells us how to live and how to treat God and man. It tells about heaven and hell. This is a divine revelation.

Many men write books of life, but the Bible is the one great, supreme Word of life. If you want to know what course of action to take, go to the Bible. It is God's Word. If you follow it you will never go wrong. A love letter is always read and treasured. The Big Book is God's love letter to His children.

III. It Is Glorious Because It Reveals the Greatest Character That Ever Crossed the Centuries

Biography is the favorite topic of many authors. They write about the lives of Napoleon, of Washington, of Lincoln, but God wrote a Book and said, "This is the life of my Son, Jesus Christ." Many great characters have loomed upon the horizon of the world; they have had their little day and passed on; but Jesus came — the great character of all time. He made His impression upon the world and that impression grows deeper with every passing century.

A man in India was making a public speech and in that speech he was criticizing certain men. Suddenly he began to talk about Jesus. The crowd yelled and soon stopped him. "You cannot say anything against Jesus," they said. No man has ever been able to say anything against Him, truthfully.

Disraeli said, "Jesus walked across Europe and changed its name to Christendom." He has changed every land He has ever touched. He is the world's greatest character, and the Bible is the Book that tells of Him.

IV. It Is Glorious Because It Reveals the Only Salvation For Man

In 1492 Columbus, with three frail ships, sailed blindly out into the Atlantic Ocean. He was seeking a new route to India, but he knew not where he would find it nor how he would find it. But when a man wants to find the way to heaven he doesn't sail out into the darkness. He has explicit directions, for here in the Bible the road is plainly marked. The simplest person in the world can find that road if he is earnest and sincere.

What does the Big Book say about salvation? It says that all have sinned; that they are hopelessly lost unless they come to the Cross; that Jesus receives all who come to Him; that He forgives them, adopts them into His family, seals them with His own blood and presents them spotless before the throne of God.

Vido Mati, a twenty-four-year-old student of Barcelona, Spain, was writing his thesis for his Doctor of Philosophy degree. In reading some old books in the library he found one by a certain philosopher. The old philosopher had left his will in this book, and the will bequeathed his property to the first man who would read the book. Vido Mati took the will to the courts, was ruled the legal heir and received an estate of $250,000. That was wonderful. But if we will earnestly read and obey the Bible, we will find something infinitely more valuable. It is impossible to place a value on forgiveness from sin, deliverance from judgment, eternal life, peace with God, comfort in the Holy Spirit and the hope of heaven. These treasures we find in the Christ to whom the Bible points us.

"There is none other name under heaven given among men, whereby we must be saved" (Acts 4:12). The Big Book is the only book in the world that reveals this salvation to us.

V. It Is Glorious Because It Has a Hopeful Message For Life After Death

Here is a great question: "Is there any life after death?" Where is the answer? Only in one place — the Bible. Why do we find that answer only in the Bible? Because God is the only One who knows about the future life. He wrote the Book and gave us our only hopeful message about life after death.

What is that message? Here it is: "I am the resurrection, and the life: he that believeth in me, though he were dead, yet shall he live" (John 11:25). "Because I live, ye shall live also" (John 14:19). "I will come again, and receive you unto myself" (John 14:3). "They shall not hunger nor thirst; neither shall the heat nor sun smite them" (Is. 49:10). The Big Book is simply telling us that if we believe in Christ, He waits for us out yonder, waits to give us in another land eternal happiness and eternal joy.

A little boy attended a certain Sunday school and church. His mother was not a Christian. She had a horror of death and would not go to church for fear she would hear something about dying. On Easter Sunday the little boy came running home with a message for her. He came joyfully into the room and cried out, "Mother, you need not be afraid to die. Jesus went through the grave and left a light behind."

She came to church with him, learned the great lesson and soon became a happy Christian. Yes, Jesus has left a light behind and we need not be afraid of death. This glorious Book has a message on the future life, for we hear it say, "Fear not, I will be with thee and bring thee into Glory."

VI. It Is Glorious Because It Keeps Its Freshness

A little girl said, "The Bible is like an orange. You can squeeze it and squeeze it and it always has more juice left." You may go to the Bible and get blessing and power from it, but you cannot exhaust it. The more you read it the more power you receive. It imparts energy, but never loses strength.

The Psalmist said, "Thy word have I hid in my heart, that I might not sin against thee" (Ps. 119:11). If we have the Bible in our hearts we have something fresh to use daily. If the heart is full of His Word the Devil cannot get in. Eve let the Devil get in and she began to doubt God's Word. If we do not fill our hearts with Him and His truths, Satan will come in and wreck our lives. Nineteen hundred years ago Jesus went up against the Devil and beat him back with the Scripture every time. The Word is just as powerful and as fresh and as helpful now as it was then.

Major Whittle was riding on a train and a skeptic wanted to argue with him about religion. The Major prayed, "Lord, I am not very good at this; help me out." The skeptic began to criticize the church and the Major quoted Scripture. Again and again the skeptic brought on his criticism and again and again the Major quoted Scripture. Finally the skeptic walked off saying, "I can't do anything with you." The Bible had won the battle. If the Bible is on your side, you will always be victorious.

You may buy a loaf of bread tomorrow and it will soon be stale. But the Bible is the bread of life; it will always be fresh and up-to-date. Cut slices from it every day and you will still have plenty of it left. When the problems of life come up you can turn to the Bible and you will find the word for your heart and it will be so appropriate that you will feel that it was written yesterday just to fit your peculiar problem.

VII. It Is Glorious Because It Changes Men and Nations

Some nations are far ahead of others and the Bible is the answer. Andrew Jackson said, "The Bible is the rock upon which our Republic rests." Horace Greeley said, "It is impossible to mentally or physically enslave a Bible reading people." "Blessed is the nation whose God is the Lord" (Ps. 33:12). With the Bible as a foundation stone a nation has some hope of progress and civilization. A Rabbi in Vienna had a son who had been taught to hate the name of Jesus and the New Testament. One day a missionary on the street corner handed this young man a book. He accepted the book, thanked the missionary for it, not knowing what it was. When he reached home he found that the book was the New Testament written in Hebrew. He stealthily took it to his room, locked the door and read it all night. In reading God's Word he became convinced that Jesus was the expected Messiah, and he became a Christian.

A native of Africa came to Dr. Moffat one day and told him that his hunting dog had eaten two pages of the Bible and therefore would be useless to him. "Why do you think so?" asked Dr. Moffat. The man replied, "I have seen fierce warriors who have been tamed by the Bible and I am afraid it will do the same for my dog." It is true that men with fierce passions have been tamed by the coming of the truths of the Bible into their hearts. A man said to me a little while ago, "I will never go back to drinking and a sinful life again. I know the difference now between that life and the Christian life." That difference was made by the truth of the Bible.

Two sisters had been absent from each other for years and then one came to visit the other one. In the meantime one of them had become a Christian. After several days the other sister said, "I don't know what has happened to you, but you are much easier to live with than you used to be." The Bible had changed her.

You read some books and enjoy them, but you do not say of them, "They have changed my life." But when you read the Bible and let its teachings enter into your heart you can say, "I have been transformed by the Word of truth."

A boy was ordered by his father to quit reading the Bible, but he slipped it aside and read it despite his father's objections. One day the father caught him reading the Bible, and immediately snatched it away from him and threw it into the fire. He noticed, however, that the boy was smiling, and said to him, "Why are you smiling?" The boy answered, "Why, I was just thinking that you cannot burn this in here," and he pointed to his heart. That is the place to keep the Bible stored.

Yes, the Bible is the greatest Book in the world and has the greatest influence. It is the world's biggest seller. But what does all this mean to you and me unless we read it and store it in our hearts? We talk about the forgotten man — here is the forgotten Book, and yet it can be the greatest blessing in life if we let it have its way in our hearts.

In the Chicago fire a man's store was destroyed. The next morning he placed a table at the front of the store and upon a sign he painted these words: "Everything lost except wife and children and hope! Business resumed tomorrow as usual."

You and I may lose everything, yet if we cling to the words of the Big Book it will be our hope to carry us through all the days that are to come and safely at last into the Haven of Rest.

9

Last of All He Sent His Son

But last of all he sent unto them his son, saying, They will reverence my son (Matthew 21:37).

In our text Jesus again assumes the role of the master storyteller. He says that a man owned a vineyard. This vineyard was up-to-date in every respect. It contained a tower and a wine press and every convenience. The owner rented this vineyard to a group of men, and when the harvest season came he sent three servants to collect the rent. But instead of collecting the rent, these servants were beaten and killed by the men to whom the vineyard had been rented. The next time the owner increased the number of servants. When this next group of servants tried to collect the rent they received the same treatment. Finally the man said, "I will send my son and surely they will reverence him." But when the husbandmen saw the son coming they said, "Aha, here is his son, let us kill him!" And they seized the son and brutally put him to death.

This was the end of the story which Jesus told. Turning to the crowd He said to them, "What do you think the Lord of the vineyard should do to these wicked men?" And the people replied, "These men should be destroyed and the vineyard rented to someone who will pay the rent."

The application here is to the Jewish nation. God had given them the Promised Land and had called them His people. He expected some fruit to come from them, but He was bound to be disappointed. He sent His prophets and they were slain. The people went on in their sin. "Last of all he sent his son" . . . and what happened to Him? "He came unto his own, and his own received him not" (John 1:11). Instead of receiving God's Son they slew Him upon a cross and God took the kingdom and gave it to the nations of the world. I will not say more of the Jewish application; rather, I will speak of the individual application of this text. Let us look at what God has done in an effort to get men to leave their sin and live for Him.

The great drama of sin and salvation began in the Garden of Eden. God put man in this garden and man sinned. Now everything that God has done since that time has been in relation to that sin and its consequences.

I. Some of God's Great Strokes

In an effort to turn men from their sin and to Himself He sent His servants to do certain things.

1. *He sent Noah and the flood and death.* The sin which began in such a small way in Eden grew until it covered the world. When God created the world He said, "It is good." But after a while He said, "I am sorry that I made man." The world needed a house cleaning and God sent a flood to cleanse it. Out of the flood He saved Noah and his family. Mankind began over again, but man had not yet learned the lesson, for soon he was going down into sin again and the effect of the flood upon the morals of the people lasted only a few years.

2. *He sent Moses and the Law and the idea of a blood sacrifice.* God's people were in slavery in Egypt and He sent Moses down to bring them out. Moses took them toward a land flowing with milk and honey. You would think they would have been eternally grateful for being released from their bondage. You would think that they would have loved God forever. But — would you believe it? — they began to sin against Him before they were one hundred miles away from the flesh pots of Egypt.

In His great love God gave them a righteous law and an idea of a blood sacrifice for sin. He instructed them in a definite method of worship and felt that if they offered the sacrifice and received the promise of forgiven sin, they would see a picture of His own great loving heart. But it was to no avail, for they went on and on in their sin.

3. *He sent David and his songs and the assurance of forgiven sins.* David came and sang, "The Lord is my shepherd" (Ps. 23:1). Again he sang, "God is our refuge and strength, a very present help in trouble" (Ps. 46:1). Over and over again he told of the greatness of the love of God and how He would care for those who put their trust in Him. Then one day the sweet singer fell into sin, but soon he had sincerely repented of that sin. God forgave him and put in his heart another song. David came back to tell how happy a man could be after God had forgiven him and in love had washed his sin away. But all the wonderful testimonies which David gave did not move the people, for they went on and on in their sin.

4. *Then He sent Jeremiah and his tears.* God knew the moving power of tears, and so He sent Jeremiah, the weeping prophet. This man went up and down the land pleading everywhere with tears in his eyes and a catch in his voice. He said, "God does love you with an everlasting love. Turn unto Him, repent of your sins and His blessings will flow down into your hearts." But even these tears did not move the people.

5. *Then He sent Isaiah and his loving invitations.* Isaiah was the greatest of the prophets and he told the people more about Jesus than any other Old Testament prophet. He went to the multitudes and cried out in God's name, "Ho, everyone that thirsteth, come ye to the waters" (Is. 55:1). Again he said, "Though your sins be as scarlet, they shall be as white as snow" (Is. 1:18). But even then the people did not heed; they went on in sin.

6. *Then He sent the kings of the earth and captivity and chastisement.* God told His people that if they sinned and went into idolatry He would send them into captivity. They lived all right for a while, but soon they were forgetting God and sinking down into sin. Then He sent the cruel kings of the earth with their mighty armies and the people were taken away in slavery. They learned many things in their captivity and many of them turned back to God. They were sent back to the land again, but soon God was again forgotten.

Every plan failed; it wasn't God's fault; it was man's fault, for we read, "The heart is deceitful above all things, and desperately wicked" (Jer. 17:9). Man continued in his sin. . . . And then the great hour struck. God made His master stroke; God did the greatest thing He ever did.

II. Last of All He Sent His Son

Here is an artist who paints many pictures. And finally he says, "I am going to paint my masterpiece." He gathers his materials together. In his mind and heart he has an ideal. He sets to work in great earnestness. Finally when he has finished he stands back and says, "It is my masterpiece." Likewise, in the fullness of time God said, "I have done all this for the world and men are still sinful. Now I have an idea in my mind which I have had since the world began. I will send my Son, my Only-begotten Son, and give Him for the world's redemption."

So Jesus came, but men crucified Him upon Calvary. As He bled His life away upon the tree, God said, "It is My final and supreme sacrifice for man. I have done all that even God can do. If men will not accept My Son as their Saviour, I must give them up to their sins and I will allow them to be lost forever."

Now why did God send His Son?

1. *God sent His Son to reveal His own heart.* Through the years people had heard about God; they had felt His

judgments; but they never knew His great heart. They never knew how much He loved them. They never knew what kind of a being He was. And so when He sent His Son He said to mankind, "Look at Jesus, My Son. Feel the warmth of His heart. See how He lives and loves and then you will know about Me, for My Son and I are One." The Bible tells us about God. Nature paints for us a beautiful picture of the Heavenly Father. But if you want a perfect picture of God you must look into the face of the Lord Jesus Christ.

2. *God sent His Son to be a picture of God's power.* Now Jesus did not bring all of God's power down to the earth with Him. He emptied Himself of a portion of it. Like a strong man with his hands tied behind his back, withholding part of his physical power, Jesus withheld a part of His spiritual power. Yet He kept some of that power and used it always for others. When He saw a blind man, He gave him his sight. To a crippled man He gave a new body. To the leper He gave cleansing. He brought the dead back to life and gave comfort and hope to broken hearts. He stilled the storms and fed the multitudes. All of this was a picture of God's power which showed how God could touch men and help them up out of their sin.

A woman who was a dope fiend became tired of living. In her hotel room she decided to commit suicide. But the radio was going and soon the voice of a minister came over the air. She heard the Gospel, called the preacher for an interview, talked with him and was saved. Instead of going to a suicide's grave she found happiness in a good Christian life. That is a picture of God's power. That is what He has been doing down through the centuries. And Jesus showed a picture of this power in His own life.

3. *God sent His Son to teach a better way of living.* He gave to man a Golden Rule. The old rule was one of retaliation; it was an "eye for an eye and a tooth for a tooth."

Man said, "If anyone harms you, you are to hurt him in return." But when Jesus came He said, "Do unto others as you would have them do unto you." Will the Golden Rule work? That isn't the question. Here is the question: Have you tried it out?

4. *God sent His Son to become a blood sacrifice.* Christ was the final sacrifice for sin. Through the years men had been offering a sacrifice upon a bloody altar. According to God's plan blood had to be spilt before sin could be forgiven. Do not criticize the preacher for talking about blood, for in Hebrews 9:22 we read: "Without shedding of blood is no remission." In I John 1:7 we read: "The blood of Jesus Christ his Son cleanseth us from all sin." Now you and I never bring a lamb nor a dove to the sacrificial altar. Why? Because Jesus became the final sacrifice. It is not necessary that more blood be spilt. In His death He made salvation possible for all men with no more sacrifice.

A missionary was working with one of the tribes down in Africa. He thought that his work had been a failure and he told the old chief that he was leaving. The chief was sad when he heard the news and called all the people together that they might hear the message of the missionary once more. The missionary told the story of Christ on the Cross. He read Matthew 26 and 27. When he had finished his reading the old chief said, "Read that again." When the missionary came to the words, "And they crucified him," the old chief leaped to his feet and cried out, "Take Him down! Take Him down from that Cross. He doesn't belong there; I belong upon that Cross!" And it is true, my friends. We have sinned and we deserve to die, but He went to the Cross and shed His blood for us and now salvation is ours through Him.

5. *God sent His Son to be a new and living Way.* The only way to get to God and heaven is through Jesus Christ, God's Son. Now men try to get to God and heaven in

various ways. This man says, "I will make my gifts large; I will pay my way. Maybe God will accept me because of my large contributions." Another man says, "By my works I will get to God. Surely if He sees me doing good works He will give me entrance into heaven." Another man says, "I will do penance. God will surely recognize that." Another man says, "I will go through the various Christian forms. I will submit to baptism and partake of the Lord's Supper and surely God will recognize these things and admit me into the heavenly home." But God says, "No, none of these things is right. You cannot climb out of your sin and up to heaven in any of these ways. There is only one way: through faith in My Son." He is the ladder from man's sins to the Father's heart. If you try to come up any other way you will fall short of the goal.

An Eastern shepherd was leading his flock along the mountainside. Two young lambs were frolicking along by their mother in the sunlight. But soon the pathway became too steep; they couldn't make it and they began to cry out piteously. The mother ran back to where they were, lingered a while and then ran on ahead, trying to lure them up the pathway. But it was in vain. They couldn't make the steep climb. The young lambs were in great danger. Even then the eagles were soaring above the cliffs, ready to pounce down upon them at the first opportunity. But in a minute the shepherd heard their cries and went back down beside them. He tenderly lifted the two lambs, put them in the great folds of his coat, and they went safely up the slope with the rest of the flock. So, my friend, you are not saved by your strength or your greatness, but you are saved by your cry for help. If you will today cry out and say, "Lord, I am lost; I am going down, help me!" then I say to you that He will take you into His arms and take you safely into heaven with the rest of the fold. Yes, He came to be a new and living Way.

6. *God will send His Son again some day.* Before Christ's first coming, God said that He would send Christ in the fullness of time. God fulfilled His Word. In the New Testament alone God tells us 318 times that His Son is coming back to the earth again. He is coming, not to live and then die, but to live and to reign forever and ever. As the promise of the first coming was fulfilled, so shall be the promise of the second coming. He did wonderful things when He was here the first time, but He will do more wonderful things when He comes the next time.

One day, and it may be sooner than we expect, the heavens will burst open and Jesus will appear in the air. All the dead who have believed in Him shall be raised up incorruptible. All the living who have believed in Him shall be changed and caught up. Both groups will go up to meet Him in the air and will never be separated from Jesus or from their loved ones. Not all the people will be taken up, but only those who have been saved. The others will be left for the Great Tribulation, the Great White Throne and the Lake of Fire. Which group will you be in? I am not asking you if you are a member of the church. I am not asking if you have made a contribution every Sunday to the church, or if you are holding an office in the church. I am asking this question: Are you His? Will you be ready when He comes?

Sometime ago I heard Evangelist Wade House tell the following story. It was Christmas Eve and a certain farmer was finishing his tasks about the farm. The weather was bitter cold and his heart was heavy as he thought of the loved one who had been gone so long. Finally he finished the chores about the farm, picked up a load of wood for the stove, took it into the house and placed it in the wood box behind the stove. His wife was putting the finishing touches on the evening meal. Soon he had washed his hands and was ready for supper. His wife called him to the table. They sat down together and he asked the blessing. As he lifted his head he looked over toward his wife and saw that her eyes were swimming with tears. "It was seven years ago tonight," she said. They had a good supper, but neither of them could eat. They nibbled at the food, but soon they had finished and the wife washed the dishes and put them away.

In a few minutes they went into the living room and sat down in their favorite chairs. He tried to read the evening paper, but somehow it did not seem to be very interesting that night. He looked into the fire and said to his wife, "It was seven years ago tonight that she left us." Then he took down the family Bible, read a chapter and offered a simple prayer. His voice broke as he prayed for his daughter who was out somewhere in the world of sin. He wound the clock, took the lamp in his hand, and they started for bed. It was a cold night and they did not put the shepherd dog out, but permitted him to sleep that night by the fireside.

Yonder in the city the pastor and a few Christians met at a certain church for a Christmas Eve service. The forlorn figure of a young woman came down the street. She had once been beautiful, but now the marks of sin were upon her face and body. She heard the singing of a Christmas hymn, and thinking that she might find a warm place to rest, opened the door and went into the church. She sat near the radiator and was soon warm and comfortable. The pastor told the old story of the coming of Jesus and quoted John 1:12: "As many as received him, to them gave he power to become the sons of God." Then the pastor gave his invitation. He said, "Is there anyone here who will come now? He will receive you if you will come to Him." The poor girl had been listening. She felt that surely the message was for her. She had sinned and her heart was broken tonight because of that sin. She went down the aisle and said to the pastor, "I have been a bad sinner, will He receive me?" The pastor replied, "Yes, He will receive anyone who comes to Him by faith. He said He would. I know He will receive you." Before the service was over the poor girl had found a Friend such as she had never known before. She went down the street and boarded the interurban train which went far out into the country. She took her remaining few coins and paid her fare. The conductor spoke a word of Christmas greeting, but the girl only smiled and said, "He will receive me; He said He would." The conductor thought that she was a bit "touched in the head" and went about his business.

Finally, far out there in the country, the girl left the train and walked for many miles through the snow toward home. When she came in sight of the home she saw that the light was still burning in the hall. It had been burning there every night for seven years just for her. She was finally able to get to the door. It wasn't locked and she turned the knob and walked inside. There was a deep growl and the old shepherd dog came toward her with his teeth bared. He did not recognize her and yet he, too, had been waiting for her for seven long years. She called his name and the dog recognized her voice and crawled over toward her. The girl came into the living room and fell down on the floor by the fireside. The old dog nestled close to her and kept her warm through the night.

On Christmas morning the farmer and his wife came down and found her there. She wasn't the beautiful young girl who had left home seven years before; the marks of sin were upon her; but she was still their daughter and they loved her with all their hearts. They believed that their prayers had been answered. The father took her up tenderly and placed her in her own bed. She smiled up into his face and said, "Daddy, He will receive me; He said He would." They gave her their sweetest and most thoughtful attention and soon she was well again. Jesus had received her, and her father and mother had received her, and she was happy.

Last of all God sent His Son. He sent Him for you and you and you. Will you receive Him, too? Will you give your heart to Him?

10

A Well — A Woman — A World

There cometh a woman of Samaria to draw water: Jesus saith unto her, Give me to drink (John 4:7).

If you turn on your radio tomorrow morning you can get the news from all over the world. You can hear voices from London, from Cairo, from Paris and from Australia. The announcer tells you to look for fuller details in the daily newspaper. Things which happened ten hours before in a place ten thousand miles away are related in that paper. But in the time of Christ there were no radios and newspapers. However, one of the best places to hear the news was at the town well. People gathered there and daily listened to the events of the world as they passed from lip to lip. In the Bible days the well was a very important place.

Now let us stop by one of these wells today and listen to a certain conversation. This well is in Samaria near the little city of Sychar. It was dug many years before by Jacob. As we stand by the well we see Jesus and His disciples approach. Jesus looks worn and tired. When He gets to the well He sits down upon the curb to rest and sends the disciples into town to buy lunch. In a moment we see a woman approaching the well. Who is she? And why does she come to the well at this hour?

I. The Samaritan Sinner

It was not the custom of the women of Sychar to come to the well at midday. They came to the well early in the morning and in the evening to draw water. Why then did this woman come at this time? She came along for another

105

purpose. She was not a good woman. Long ago she had sold her virtue as merchandise in the market of lust, and it is possible that she came seeking a man. She was plying her trade. She was engaged in the oldest profession in the world.

Yet the worst sinners often long for a better life. They have gone down the whole way of sin; they know that sin doesn't pay and doesn't satisfy. They long for something that really satisfies. They need Christ more than anything else. It is often easier to reach a poor deep-dyed sinner than a self-righteous moral sinner. The poor sinner knows there must come some change to him, but the self-righteous man trusts in his own goodness and goes on down to an eternal doom.

Charlotte Elliott asked a man how she could become a Christian and he replied, "It is very simple. Just come to Jesus." "But," said she, "I am a great sinner. Will He take me just as I am?" "Yes," answered the man, "He will take you just as you are and no other way." "If He will take me just as I am," she said, "then I will come to Him." She came to Jesus and was saved. Later on she wrote the beautiful words:

> Just as I am, without one plea,
> But that Thy blood was shed for me,
> And that Thou bidd'st me come to Thee,
> O Lamb of God, I come, I come!

Whether you are good or bad, rich or poor, this is the only way. If you are a sinner as this woman was, *come to Him just as you are,* and He will fill your life with joy and happiness and hope.

II. A Seeking Saviour

At the well the sinful woman meets the seeking Saviour. Now there is a divine purpose in this meeting. We read, "He must needs go through Samaria" (John 4:4). That was not the usual route. The Jews had no dealings with the Samaritans. They felt that they were polluted if their feet touched the country of Samaria. They went a round-about way from Judea to Galilee. Then why did Jesus go the direct way? He went because of the woman who was there, the woman who needed to be saved, who needed the touch which would bring eternal life to her and her city. From the foundation of the world it must have been God's plan for her to meet Christ there and be saved.

There are no accidents in God's program. He never makes a mistake. A preacher started to a distant town to hold a meeting. He missed his train and became greatly distressed because he could not reach the town in time for the first service. In the paper the next morning he read that the train had been wrecked and that many lives had been lost. He thanked God then that he had missed that train. He reached the town a little later and God used him mightily for the salvation of many souls. Yes, God often changes our ways for our best good. He changes our disappointments to His appointments.

Now look at Jesus' tactful approach to this woman. He speaks to her, saying, "Give me to drink" (John 4:7). This is a very neighborly request. It is filled with simplicity, but that is just like Jesus. He knows that this is a good way to get acquainted with the woman. My car stalled in front of my house sometime ago and my neighbor came out with his car and pushed me down the street. Since then there has been a warm neighborly feeling between us. In like manner Jesus approaches this woman in a tactful and neighborly way, by simply asking for a drink of water.

The woman is quick to reply: "How is it that thou . . . askest drink of me . . . the Jews have no dealing with the Samaritans" (John 4:9). But Jesus breaks down the barriers of race. She may be a hated Samaritan to His people, but to Him she is a needy soul longing for the better life. To Jesus there is no East nor West, no North nor South. To Him there is no Jew nor Gentile, no bond nor free, no rich nor poor — He loves us all. Let there be one anywhere hungering and thirsting for righteousness and Jesus is the seeking, compassionate, neighborly Saviour for that one.

Jesus says to her, "If thou knewest the gift of God, and who it is that saith to thee, Give me to drink; thou wouldest have asked of him, and he would have given thee living water" (John 4:10). She is thirsty for that water but she does not know that here is One who can satisfy every longing of her lonely heart.

Oh, lost man, if thou knewest the gift of God, today you would seek Him with your whole heart! If you only knew that your sin will take you to an everlasting doom, if you only knew how sweet it is to be saved and to have your sins forgiven, and how happy He can make you here and what a wonderful heaven He has prepared for His children, surely today, today, you would turn away from your sin and come to this wonderful Saviour!

Our churches are filled with nominal Christians. They are members of the church and that is about all. Oh, if they only knew the joy of a fully surrendered Christian life! Their lives are counting for the world and not for Christ. If they only knew how much happier they could be, how much more useful they could be and how much more life could mean to self and to others, and to Christ, they would bow their heads today and say, "I am not content just to be a church member. From now on Christ will have my very best."

Sometime ago I read a book about Mr. R. G. LeTourneau's life. The title of the book is, *God Runs My Business.* There isn't a more successful, nor happier, nor more useful man in America today than Mr. LeTourneau. He knows what it means to go all the way with Christ. Why not let Jesus run your business? Why not let Him run your whole life? He is deeply interested in you and you will never find a better partner.

Oh, if you knew! If you knew! If you knew! If you knew what Christ could do in your life and through your life, you would give your whole self to Him today and go out to serve Him with your full heart.

Jesus next begins the work of a skilled surgeon, as He talks to this woman. As He tells her of the Water of Life that He can give, she cries out, "Sir, give me this water, that I thirst not" (John 4:15). She does not see Him then as a Saviour; she thinks of Him only as someone who can give her something. The crowd once followed Him for the loaves and fishes. In China those who follow the missionaries simply for material advantages are called "rice Christians."

But Jesus is the real surgeon of the soul. First, He must probe the cancer of old sin and bring this woman to feel the burden of this thing which is wrong in her life; so He bluntly commands, "Go, call thy husband" (John 4:16). Then she makes an honest confession, "I have no husband" (John 4:17). Jesus commends her for her frankness and truthfulness: "Thou hast well said . . . for thou hast had five husbands; and he whom thou now hast is not thy husband" (John 4:17-18). Jesus finds something good even in the worst of sinners. We would do well to practice the same thing. There was a woman once who had a good word for everyone. One of her children said one day, "Mother, you would even say something good about the Devil." And she replied, "Well, you must admire his perseverance; he is always on the job." Many people look upon the bad instead of the good. Someone may do a thousand fine things and only one thing which is not so good, and the critics will pounce upon that one thing, criticize the person severely and forget the thousand good things. Jesus was never like that.

But the woman evades the issue. When Jesus begins to talk to her about her sin she tries to change the subject. She says, "Sir, I perceive that thou art a prophet. Our fathers worshipped in this mountain" (John 4:19-20). This is true of human nature. When men are brought face to face with their sin, they immediately say, "Let's talk about something else."

This woman has another failing. When she sees Jesus drawing her face to face with a spiritual issue she begins to talk about her father's religion. Today there are many people who are resting upon the religion of their fathers and mothers. I say to someone, "Are you a Christian?" and they answer, "My mother was a good Christian, and my father was a deacon in the church." My friend, this will not help you. This will not save your soul. The issue is between you and God.

A pastor's heart is often burdened as he sees fine Christian women whose husbands are not believers in Christ. I would have just a word of advice for these women: Be more faithful to Christ and to your church; keep sweet in your home; don't rail and ridicule; but pray for your husband and try to win him to Christ. Don't stay at home on Sunday night, but be faithful to your church services and let him know that your religion means something to you. In this way you will have an influence stronger than a thousand sermons.

Now this woman expresses the longing of a hungry heart. As Jesus talks to her the old, old longing comes to the surface and with pathos in her voice she says, "I know that Messias cometh" (John 4:25). How did she know He was coming? Probably as a girl she had heard the Scriptures read and had thus heard of Him. Her people had talked about the Messiah and longed for Him and looked for His coming. There are many hungry hearts about us today. They are longing for His coming to bless their lives. They are hungering for what He alone can give. Are you telling them about Him?

You may not be able to talk to people about their relationship to Christ, but you can at least invite them to your church to hear the Gospel. What about your grocer or the boy who brings your paper, or the man from whom you buy your milk? Here are these opportunities all around you every day. Hungry hearts are longing for the light, and you and I have the matchless opportunity of telling them about Jesus.

A fine young man said to me the other day: "My neighborhood is filled with people who do not go to church. Even if it makes me unpopular, I am going to try to win these neighbors to Christ and the church." Think what it would mean if every member of our church went out and tried to win those around them to Christ and His Church.

III. The Revealing Redeemer

The woman expressed her longing to see the Messiah. Immediately Jesus reveals Himself. He says, "I that speak unto thee am he" (John 4:26). And what does she do? She opens up her heart and Jesus walks in to transform her and save her forevermore.

She leaves her old life of sin. She leaves her water pot at the well and bounds back on happy feet to the city of Sychar. This is symbolic of the way she leaves her old life. This is the natural change that comes to those who trust Christ. When He comes into your life you are changed into a new creature. Every genuinely converted person lives a different life when Christ comes into his heart.

This woman becomes a Spirit-filled servant. The longing of her heart is satisfied; she has found Jesus and she wants others to know the joy that is hers. We read that she goes back into the city and gives her testimony. When the people hear about it, they flock out to the well and fall in love with Jesus. That is a natural sequence. When our own souls find joy in Him we want others to know Him too.

IV. The Waiting World

The disciples soon come back to the well and Jesus tells them that he doesn't want anything to eat. They begin to ask one another, "Hath any man brought him ought to eat?" (John 4:33). And Jesus answers, "I have meat to eat that ye know not of. . . . My meat is to do the will of him that sent me, and to finish his work" (John 4:32, 34). Then He looks down toward the city and thinks of the woman who has opened her heart to Him. He is thinking of her as typifying the lost people of all the world. So He says to His disciples: "Lift up your eyes, and look on the fields; for they are white already unto harvest" (John 4:35). He is thinking of all the thousands who are lost in the world and of His desire for their salvation.

Jesus was waiting by the well. The people in Sychar were waiting. The woman came to the well and took back with her, not a pot of water, but the Water of Life which refreshes eternally. My friends, this woman had only a limited knowledge of Jesus, yet she won a whole city to Him. You and I stand nineteen hundred years this side of her; we have more knowledge of the Saviour than she had. Are we doing what she did? Are we making our lives count for Him? Are we surrendering our broken lives to Him as she did? Are we asking Him to use us as He used her?

In 1931 a homing pigeon was released in France. The home loft of that pigeon was in Indo-China, 7,200 miles away. The bird flew three hundred miles per day and in twenty-four days reached Indo-China. If such a little bird with the limited power which God has given it can do a thing like that, how much more should you and I do with the great powers which God has given us? Yes, we have the talents and the power to bring men to His feet if we will only let Him have His way with us.

Nineteen hundred years ago a man went out to die upon a Cross. Why? Because someone was lost Today a little group of faithful Christian people come together and organize a church. Why? Because someone is lost. And now that church has its preaching services, prayer meetings, Sunday school and the other services. Why? Because someone is lost! Someone is lost!

Oh, my friends, we are in the world to win the lost; we are in business here for God. Won't you line up with Him? Won't you surrender to Christ? Won't you say, "From now on I will live for Him who died for me"?

11

Why Every Christian Should Tithe

> Bring ye all the tithes into the storehouse, that there may be meat in mine house, and prove me now herewith, saith the Lord of hosts, if I will not open you the windows of heaven, and pour you out a blessing, that there shall not be room enough to receive it (Malachi 3:10).

I had just begun my ministry in a small church in North Carolina. In that church there was a certain man who made an excellent salary, but he gave only one dollar per month to the church. One day he said to a friend of his, "I like our new preacher because he never preaches about money." Just about that time I preached two sermons about the Biblical method of giving. This man immediately quit coming to church. The Gospel and the Bible meant nothing to him. He was not seeking the Lord's will for his life. He just wanted to be entertained and left alone.

But in another pastorate a young couple who worked in a flower shop began to tithe after I had preached on the matter of Scriptural giving. They received such a blessing out of tithing and God was so good to them that they simply felt they had to show their appreciation for my teaching on tithing. Every year they sent me a big bouquet of red roses to commemorate the anniversary of their beginning to tithe. Now this young couple owns a large flower shop of their own. God always blesses a tither.

I make no apology for preaching on the matter of Scriptural giving. There is more in the Bible about giving than there is about heaven or hell. God was the first giver, He was the Great Giver. He wants us to be like Him. He wants us to give. Now this matter of giving comes mighty close to our hearts and lives, but I feel that I would not be preaching all the counsel of God if I did not preach on tithing. In writing to the Corinthians, Paul said, "I fear that I have sinned against you by not preaching about giving." Money is a vital part of human life. Money is a part of self. It represents our brain and our brawn, our time and our talents. The preacher ought to preach on vital things, the things that touch everyday life. Therefore, he ought to preach on Scriptural giving.

There are many troubles which come up in our churches over the matter of money. But if we can get our people to be stewards and to give their money in the right spirit to the Lord, this trouble will be dissolved. The average man will go to church and take an active part and a greater interest in the church if he is putting his money there. Here is a man who invests five thousand dollars in a store. He doesn't go away and leave this store to run itself; he has his money there and he is interested in the welfare of the business. So if we can get men to give as they should, and as the Bible teaches, they will show a deeper interest in the church and many of our problems will be solved.

God has given us directions as to our giving. If we are His we want to follow His will. He tells us that we are to tithe. When I was in the seminary I had two half-time churches. One Saturday before I started my journey to one of these churches, a fellow student asked me what I was going to preach about on Sunday morning. I replied that I was going to preach on the matter of giving the tithe. "No," said he, "you are going to preach on the matter of paying the tithe." He was exactly right. We do not give God anything when we pay the tithe. It already belongs to Him. We are not making a gift; we are simply paying an honest debt.

The real consecrated Christian wants to do the will of

God. The indifferent Christian cares nothing about God's will. Many good Christians do not tithe because they do not understand the Biblical teaching concerning tithing. I believe that if you show a consecrated Christian God's will in this matter, he will say, "That's the right thing to do and I will do it." In James 4:17 we read: "Therefore to him that knoweth to do good, and doeth it not, to him it is sin." We sin when we know the will of God about our giving and refuse to enter into that will.

One of my deacons said on one occasion: "There is only one way in which I can do the will of God perfectly and that is in my giving." We fall short of His perfect will in many things, but by bringing our tithes and offerings to be used for His glory, we know we can at least do His will perfectly in this matter. Now why should a Christian tithe?

I. The Bible Teaches It

Now this ought to be a sufficient reason. If the Bible tells us to do a thing, we ought to do it. We believe the Bible teachings on other subjects — why not accept its teachings on the matter of tithing?

Tithing is surely taught in the Old Testament. There are some who say that the tithe belongs to the Mosaic Law, and that this Law has been done away with. However, I would remind you that the Bible spoke of tithing four hundred years before Moses came into the world. Abraham paid tithes to Melchizedek and this was long before the day of Moses. When Jacob had his famous vision at Bethel, he said, "Of all that thou shalt give me I will surely give the tenth unto thee" (Gen. 28:22). This was before the day of Moses. In later years when Jacob returned to Bethel, God had richly blessed him and made him a wealthy man. Did his tithing have anything to do with it? In Leviticus 27:30 we read: "And all the tithe of the land, whether of the seed of the land, or of the fruit of the tree, is the Lord's:

it is holy unto the Lord." All the way through the Old Testament we find that when God's people were in harmony with God, they were faithful in paying their tithe.

Tithing is definitely taught in the New Testament. While the ceremonial law of animal sacrifices was discontinued and nailed to the Cross, we have no evidence that tithing was abolished. Surely Jesus must have been a tither. He said that He came not to destroy, but to fulfil the Law. If the Jew under the Law, knowing not the freedom which we enjoy in Christ, felt that he should tithe, how much more should we who know Christ as a blessed Saviour.

Jesus is the supreme authority on all matters of life and death. In Matthew 23:23 He told the people of His day that they ought to tithe. In the Book of Acts we find the people giving far more than a tithe. They sold their possessions and brought the proceeds to the apostles to be used for the work of the church. Paul commended the Macedonian Christians for giving out of their deep poverty. They gave far more than the tithe. The average Christian today is not a wealthy person. If he pays the tithe he is not therefore giving out of his wealth. The majority of people who tithe are not wealthy people in the things of this world, but they are wealthy in the matter of loving Christ and desiring to do His will.

One day Christ was standing over against the treasury. The big men of His day came and made their large gifts. Jesus had no word for them. But when the widow came up and gave her little bit, He said that she had given all that she had. This was another example of one who gave beyond the tenth.

Do you believe the Bible? Surely you do. Then you ought to obey its teachings. You believe what it says about creation, about salvation, about baptism and the Lord's Supper and many other things. Then you ought to believe the Bible on tithing and you ought to tithe because the Bible teaches it.

II. God Is Good

Jeremiah said, "[The Lord's mercies] are new every morning" (Lam. 3:22, 23). Surely God has been mighty good to everyone of us. Think of how He has blessed you down through the years. He has blessed you with good health, a good home, a nice family, good friends, and many, many other marvelous blessings. Every one of us ought to say, "Dear Lord, because of Thy goodness to me, I know that I ought to give my best to Thee." The goodness of God ought to make us obey Him. Here is a man who rents a farm from its owner. The owner supplies the equipment, the stock, the land and the houses. It is only right that he should receive some return from the land at the end of the year. Well, isn't it that way with Christians? God has supplied us with everything that we have. Are we going to soak it all up like a sponge and give nothing in return for all of His blessings?

"But," you say, "I worked hard; I made this money; I built this house." But it was God who gave you the power to do it all. Without Him, you would have no health, no strength, no breath. Surely because of His goodness you ought to give Him at least one-tenth of all that you earn.

III. Believers Will Suffer Loss If They Do Not Tithe

In the Book of Malachi God tells the people that they are going to be cursed with a curse. Why? Simply because they are not tithing; they are robbing God. If they think God is an old softie and that they can go on their way, doing as they please, they are greatly mistaken. When God commands His children to do a certain thing, His children will surely be punished if they are not obedient.

If we do not pay God His tithe, He really knows how to collect it another way. But there is no joy if He must take it away from us through sickness or trouble. A certain farmer made a pledge to his church. When he had harvested his crops, he paid his grocery bill, his seed bill, his fertilizer bill, and all of his other debts. But he did not pay his pledge to God. One night his barn burned to the ground, causing the loss of a large part of his crop and two of his horses. The next day the farmer went to the bank, borrowed some money and paid his pledge to the Lord. He felt that God was punishing him for his disobedience. Can anyone say that the farmer was wrong in feeling this way?

Some years ago I had dinner one day with a fine Christian couple. They lived on a farm and raised cotton as their money crop. They told me that they were tithers, always giving God the first fruits of the increase of their land. A strange thing happened that year. These people had a wonderful crop, but the farmer on the adjoining farm made an absolute failure of his crop. The soil on both farms was of the same type; the same kind of seed had been planted and the same amount of labor had been given to both farms. Yet one piece of ground was almost barren and the other brought forth much fruit. Did God have anything to do with it? Did tithing have anything to do with it? I think that it did.

Do you think that you are greater than God? Do you think that you can do as you please with His money, and get away with it? No, my friends, it costs you something not to tithe. It is expensive to disobey the Lord. Maybe you are having a hard time right now. Maybe you can't pay your debts. This may be the answer: you are not giving God a chance to bless you by being obedient to Him.

IV. It Pays To Tithe

"But," you say, "preacher, that is a selfish and greedy way to put it." But you must remember that God is the One who makes the promise. He said that He would pay those who tithe. He attaches a blessing to every command. "Him that cometh to me I will in no wise cast out" (John 6:37). This is His promise to the unsaved. "Seek ye first the kingdom of God, and his righteousness; and all these things shall be added unto you" (Matt. 6:33). This is His promise to the Christian.

God blesses the tither materially. I realize that this is a lesser blessing, but it is a blessing nevertheless. Let us think about Jacob again. When he left home, he had nothing but his staff and the little lunch his mother had prepared for him. We are told that when he returned to Bethel later he had twelve companies. He was a wealthy man. He would tell you that it paid to tithe. It is said that John D. Rockefeller carried a little worn black book with him all the time. One day he showed this book to a preacher. The first entry showed that his first income was five dollars, and it also showed that he had given one-tenth of that to the Lord. In the book there were many other entries showing that he had made millions, and given millions to the cause of Christ. He would say that it paid to tithe.

When William Colgate was a young man, he decided to leave home and seek his fortune in New York City. On the morning that he left home, he met an old friend of the family. He told this friend that he was going to New York City to become a soap maker. The old man said to him, "William, someone is going to be the best soap maker in America, and you can be that one. If you will work hard, serve the Lord faithfully and pay Him His tithe, God will give you great success." Young William promised that he would do just that. The years went by and the promise was kept. Colgate became one of the great men of America and gave away millions of dollars before he died. He would say that it pays to tithe.

Many lesser lights could give the same testimony. I have been keeping books with the Lord since I entered the ministry many years ago. My salary the first month was $42.00, but I have given God His part down through the years and He has prospered me in a wonderful way until now I have learned the joy of giving much more than the tithe.

There is never any depression with the Lord; He will take care of you if you look after His interests. Everyone who has faithfully tithed for any period of time could testify as to the blessings received, and certainly no true tither would ever go back to any other system of giving.

It is simply a matter of trusting God. If you will give Him the first tenth, He will certainly make the other nine-tenths go farther. Why not launch out upon His promises? Tell Him: "I do believe Thy promises. I'm going to do my part and I know that Thou wilt do Thy part." Maybe you are in debt and you feel that you ought to pay off those debts. I never heard of a tither who didn't pay his debts. It is just a matter of trusting God. It is just a matter of doing your part, then watching God pour out the blessings upon you.

Listen to II Corinthians 9:6: "He which soweth sparingly shall also reap sparingly; and he which soweth bountifully shall reap also bountifully." Listen to God as in the Book of Malachi He calls upon men to test Him. He says that He will pour out such a blessing that you will not be able to receive it. But this blessing is dependent upon your tithing. Just think of it! The great God of heaven owns everything and He tells a little man down here to try Him out, to see if He will not give Him a blessing. You cannot afford not to take God up on this promise. Maybe you work for some large corporation. You do your part and you trust the corporation to pay you at the end of the month. Can't you trust God the same way? If you do your part He will certainly take care of you.

It also pays spiritually to tithe. That is the reason God wants you to tithe: He wants you to grow in grace. You will never grow in grace as long as you withhold from God that which rightfully belongs to Him. God wants to bless your life and your giving. He wants to make you a better person and a stronger Christian. Tithing is one of His means of grace. Can you say, "I am doing as God teaches; I am having a part in His great plan"?

I have heard many preachers say this: "The most consecrated and the most faithful people in my church are the tithers." Proverbs 11:25 tells us that the liberal soul shall be made fat. Certainly you don't want to be a lean Christian. You will be a better Christian, have a clearer conscience, and experience the joy of soul-growth if you will obey God in the matter of tithing.

V. BELIEVERS MUST ACCOUNT FOR THEIR MONEY TO GOD SOMEDAY

Jesus tells us the parable of the talents. When the master went away, he gave one talent to the first servant, two talents to the next one and five talents to the third servant. When the master came back the servants were called to give an account of the way they had used the money. Our Lord has gone away in the heavens, but He is coming back someday. He has said to us: "Occupy until I come" (Luke 19:13). When He comes back, we must give an account to Him of the way we have handled our money. In Deuteronomy 8:18 we read that it is God who giveth us the power to get wealth. Since He has given us this power, He is going to call us to account to Him someday. Some years ago I served as trustee of a small college. I did not own the college, I simply acted with the other trustees in administering its affairs. Once each year we had to go before the State Convention and give an account of our trusteeship. It is the same way with our money. We do not own that which we possess for a while. We are simply stewards or trustees. Someday we must account to God for this stewardship.

Paul says, "I am a debtor" (Rom. 1:14). We belong in the same category. We owe the Gospel of Christ to every creature in the world. If we withhold our tithe and thus rob men of the glorious message of the Gospel, their blood will be upon our hands as we stand before God's great judgment bar.

God says that the man who does not tithe robs God. I did not say it; God said it. I would not like to be hailed into a court of this world and be accused of robbing someone. But I would rather this happen than to stand before the judgment seat and have it said of me that I robbed God. When we do not tithe we rob God of that which belongs to Him; we rob others of the blessing which our money could bring to them; we rob ourselves of the joy that can come only to those who seek to follow the will of God.

In a certain church a pastor had poured out his heart for the cause of missions. At the close of the sermon a special offering was taken for foreign missions. The well-dressed people in the congregation sat there in their smug complacency and dropped their offerings into the plate. Not one of them made a sacrifice. Not one of them would miss the money they gave that day. But when one of the ushers reached the back pew a strange thing happened. A little crippled girl who had no money had been greatly moved by the pastor's message. She wanted to give her best for Christ and a lost world. Since she could give no money, she decided to give the only valuable thing she had. She lifted up her crutches and laid them across the offering plate. The usher didn't know anything to do except to bring the offering plate back down to the front. When the pastor saw the little crutches, he knew the story. Taking up the crutches and holding them in his hand, he told the people of the real sacrifice this little girl was making out of her love for Christ and a lost world. Immediately the congregation was quickened into action. The people asked that they be allowed to give large sums of money in order that the crutches might be given back to the little girl. The offering plates were soon filled with a worthy offering for the Saviour.

But let me tell you of another One who gave His all for

us. On Calvary's Cross our Saviour made the supreme sacrifice in order to save us from our sins and gain entrance to heaven for our souls. He did not stop short of the Cross; He gave all that He had. We ought to be ashamed if we are willing to give less than our best. We should never stop short of giving what God asks us to give. May God help us to see this matter of tithing in the right light, and may we say from the depths of our hearts, "God helping us, from this day forward, we will certainly do the Lord's will in the matter of our giving."

12

Climbing to Hell

The Lord is . . . not willing that any should perish, but that all should come to repentance (II Peter 3:9).

We can easily see from this text that God does not want to see a single person lost. He does not want anyone to go through this life without Christ and then go down to hell at the end of the way. He wants everyone to be saved. He is a great, loving, Heavenly Father and He has prepared a wonderful heaven for all who will put their faith in His Son. That heaven is big enough for everyone who ever lived, and God wants everyone to come and enjoy that heaven forever. Today He wants to see you saved. He is knocking at the door of your heart; He is pleading for you to come unto Him and have your sins washed away.

It is the height of foolishness for any man to reject Christ and pay the penalty of sin in everlasting death. There is every reason in the world why you should be a Christian. Look around you and you see that this world cannot permanently satisfy you. It has nothing good and lasting about it. Look out yonder into the far future and you see that the reward of the just is sure and the punishment of the wicked is everlasting. Yes, there is every reason in the world why you should be a Christian.

But it seems that some people are determined to go to hell. Here is a man who is fine in business. A problem comes up which means very little to him in dollars and cents, but he is willing to sit down and think the whole thing out in a logical way. At the same time, however, that man passes Christ by, never pondering the question: "For what shall it profit a man, if he shall gain the whole world, and lose his own soul?" (Mark 8:36).

Another man may be very wonderful in his home. A matter may come up which affects the happiness of his family and he is willing to sit down and think the matter through, that added happiness may come to his family. Yet, at the same time this man who is so fine in his earthly home gives no thought to the home beyond the sky. Yes, men give attention to everything else in the world, but give no thought and attention to Christ and salvation and the life to come. Yet God loves them and wants to save them.

Some people are so determined to go to hell that they will climb over mountains in order to get there. We could understand it if it were easy to go to hell, but it is certainly not an easy thing. It is hard to go to hell. God has put many things in the pathway of the sinner to keep him from being lost. God has erected mountains over which the sinner must climb before he can go to hell. Today I want to speak to you about some of these mountains which men must climb over in order to get to hell.

I. THE MOUNTAIN OF THE CHURCH

A man must climb over every evangelically sound church he has ever seen in order to get to hell. Why do we have our churches in every city and village and in every part of the country? They are there so that men can go and hear the Gospel and find their way to Christ. If every man in America did his duty, every man could be saved, for every man in America is within reach of a church where the saving knowledge of Christ is preached and taught. I would not like to go to hell from some desert island or from the jungles of the Congo, but I would rather go to hell from these places than from America. "Unto whomsoever much is given, of him shall be much required" (Luke 12:48). The people in America have been given much in the way of spiritual instruction, and if they go to hell their punishment will be greater because their opportunities have been greater. The church never saves anyone, but it is the agency which has cradled the Gospel and brought it down to us today. Yes, my friend, if you live and die and go down to hell, you can look back and say, "I climbed over every gospel church I ever saw in order to get here."

II. The Mountain of Gospel Sermons

Why does God call preachers and send them out into the world? He calls them so that others can hear the Gospel and find their way to Christ. You cannot go to hell without climbing over the sermons you have heard. Jesus preached the greatest sermons the world has ever heard, yet men rejected His truth and rejected Him. Because of this, their wails are filling every corner of hell today. One hundred years from now, if you are in hell it will be because you climbed over the sermons that you heard. The great sermons of the New Testament were preached by Jesus, by John the Baptist, by John and Peter. We find this warning in all of their sermons: "Repent of your sins and turn to Christ and salvation will be yours." Everyone of them preached repentance and faith. In the right kind of church today you hear the same message. But if you live and die and go down to hell, you can look back and say, "I climbed over every sermon I ever heard in order to get here."

III. The Mountain of God's Book

Every Bible in the world is a blockade between your soul and hell. You cannot go to hell without climbing over its truth.

In the olden days two prominent men decided that they would write a book against the Bible, maintaining that it was an untrustworthy guide for the hearts of men. They separated for some time in order to make their study of the subject. They planned to come together at a certain time and collaborate in writing their book against the Bible. At the given time they met at the appointed place. One man said, "I am sorry that I made that bargain with you. When I began to study the Bible I saw that I was a poor, lost sinner, and I have given my heart to Christ."

The other man said, "I, too, have found Him as my Saviour. When I began to study the conversion of Saul, I saw that I was the chief of sinners, and I have yielded my life to the Lord."

Then the other one said, "We have been living against the Book; from now on let us live by it."

When anyone decides that he is going to live by the Bible, he will soon find his way to Christ and everlasting life.

Now, you can read the Bible in a critical way, seeking to find in it some mistake or contradiction, and you will get no blessing from it. But if you will read the Bible with an earnest heart, the Holy Spirit will shine across its pages and point you to the Saviour. Every man in the world can own a Bible. Churches and Christians and Bible societies will be glad to furnish anyone with God's Word. You are without excuse. If you live and die and go down to hell, you can look back and say, "I climbed over every Bible I ever saw in order to get here."

IV. The Mountain of Conscience

God has given us a conscience which rings out and tells us when we are doing the wrong thing. Surely every man's conscience at some time tells him that he should not go on in sin, that he should turn to Christ and live his life for the Lord. A man must climb over these impressions before he can get to hell.

In my first pastorate I baptized a man seventy-two years of age. He said this to me, "I have lived in sin for seventy-two years, but every time I did anything wrong my conscience condemned me and told me that I should not have done it."

You cannot get away from your consience. It lashes like a whip and burns like a hot iron. So if you live and die and go to hell, you can look back and say, "I climbed over my conscience in order to get here."

V. The Mountain of Better Judgment

Every man's better judgment tells him that he ought to come to Christ and that he ought to come now. He knows that someday he must die and face God's judgment. In the depths of his heart he knows that it is the safe and sane and sensible thing to be a Christian.

A certain preacher wanted to win a businessman to Christ. One afternoon he went to this businessman's office and said to him, "If you could buy this corner lot today for five hundred dollars and sell it tomorrow for five thousand dollars, what would you do?"

"Why," replied the man, "you know what I would do. I would buy the lot today and sell it tomorrow and make the forty-five hundred dollars profit."

Then the preacher said, "What is there within you which tells you to do this thing?"

The man replied, "My better judgment tells me to do it. My better judgment tells me to give up the small thing in order that I might gain the big thing."

Then the preacher pressed upon the man's heart the claims of Christ, telling him that he ought to give up the little things of the pleasures of this world in order that he might gain the big thing of everlasting life. If you live and die and go down to hell, you will be forced to say this: "I did not have to come here. I climbed over my better judgment in order to get here."

VI. The Mountain of a Mother's Love and Prayers

Many of us can remember how our mothers loved us and prayed for our salvation. It may be that some of you are still living today because of the prayers of a godly mother.

You must climb over her love and prayers and tears in order to get to hell.

A boy was leaving his country home and going to live in a sinful city. Before he left, his mother said to him: "Son, you are going to live in a wicked city, but I want you to remember this: every night at nine o'clock I will be kneeling here by the bedside and praying for you."

The boy went on to the city and soon he had forgotten his mother's promise. One night he swung down the street with a group of his companions. They went into a saloon and ordered their drinks. Just as the bartender pushed the drinks across the counter, the clock on the wall chimed out nine times. The boy pushed his drink back and started out the door. When one of his companions called out to him, he simply said one word, the word "mother." Soon he had gone back to his mother and to his mother's God. Ah, yes, many a boy has been pulled back from the world and from sin by the love and prayers of a consecrated mother. If you live and die and go down to hell, you must say, "I climbed over my mother's love and prayers and tears in order to get here."

VII. The Mountain of the Sorrows and Shadows of Life

God uses everything to bring us to Himself. Even the dark providences of life are instruments in His hand to teach us of the shortness of life and of our desperate need of Him.

Some years ago I was eating supper in the home of a preacher friend in Atlanta, Georgia. The telephone rang and it was someone asking this preacher friend to conduct a funeral the next afternoon. He had another engagement and could not perform this service. I promised him that I would conduct the funeral for him. I went down to the funeral home the next afternoon and confronted a sad family. The little four-year-old boy in the home had been playing with his marbles on the sidewalk. One of the marbles eluded him and rolled out into the street. He rushed out to get his marble; he did not see the streetcar coming. The motorman did not see the little boy, and in a few minutes the poor little fellow was crushed to death under the grinding wheels of the car.

When I went in to see the family I learned that the mother almost worshiped this little boy, but she did not know Christ; she was not a Christian. She lacked the comfort that only He could give. I spoke in the funeral service as tenderly as I could. I told them that perhaps God had taken the little one on to heaven that the older ones might follow. I told them that God had taken the little lamb across the stream that the sheep might follow. I told them that the little boy would be waiting yonder in heaven with Jesus for the other members of the family and that they should give their hearts to Christ, for He alone could give comfort for this world and hope for the world to come.

In a little while we had laid the lifeless form of the child in the grave. As we turned away, the mother came and took my hand in both of hers and said to me, "Brother Ford, I know now why God allowed my little boy to be taken away. I have never given my heart to Christ, but I promise you that next Sunday morning I will go to church and I will confess Christ as my Saviour. I want to see Him someday, and I want to see my little boy again."

I wonder if somewhere along the span of the years God did not speak to you in this way. He did it because He loved you and He was trying to get to your heart. Do not turn a deaf ear to these pleadings of a great Heavenly Father. But if you live and die and go down to hell, you must say: "I climbed over the shadows and sorrows of life in order to get here."

VIII. THE MOUNTAIN OF GOD'S HOLY SPIRIT

Today the Holy Spirit stands between every man and hell. You must climb over all of His wooings and pleadings before you can go to hell. You go to church, the music stirs your heart and the sermon grips your soul. You see yourself as a poor lost sinner before God. When the invitation hymn is sung you feel a strange tug at your heart. You feel that you ought to walk down and turn away from your sin and confess Christ as your Saviour. From whence cometh that tug? Who puts such a feeling in your heart? It is none other than God's Holy Spirit. God has sent Him down to earth to convict men "of sin, and of righteousness and of judgment." If you go to hell, you must climb over the Spirit of God in order to get there.

Why am I here preaching to you today? I am here because a long time ago God's Spirit knocked at the door of my heart and I opened the door and let Christ come in and be my Saviour. And then on another occasion, He knocked again and called me to be a preacher of the Gospel. I am here today because of the work of the Holy Spirit in my heart.

Where are you going to be a hundred years from now? Where are you going to be a thousand years from now? Where are you going to be a million years from now? It all depends upon the answer which you give to the Holy Spirit. Say "yes" to Him; open up your heart; let Jesus come in and wash away your sins. All of your future happiness and all of your hope for eternity rests upon the answer that you give to the Holy Spirit. But if you live and die and go down to hell, you must say, "I am here because I climbed over the mountain of God's Holy Spirit to get here."

IX. THE MOUNTAIN OF CALVARY

The last mountain over which you have to climb to get to hell is the mountain of Calvary, upon which is the crucified Christ. Christ stands between you and the yawning pits of hell. In order to get to hell a man must climb over the Son of God; you must reject Him; you must say "no" to all of His entreaties. Today He knocks at the door of your heart. Today He says, "Come now, and let us reason together . . . though your sins be as scarlet, they shall be as white as snow" (Is. 1:18). Today He says, "He that believeth on the Son hath everlasting life; and he that believeth not the Son shall not see life; but the wrath of God abideth on him" (John 3:36). Today He says, "Come unto me, all ye that labour and are heavy laden, and I will give you rest" (Matt. 11:28). Today He says, "Him that cometh to me I will in no wise cast out" (John 6:37).

Oh, my friend, come unto Him this day; give your heart and life to Him. Do not trample Him under foot, do not climb over Jesus, for the destiny of those who reject Him is nothing but an endless hell.

But men seem to say, "I do not care; I am going to live for this life and this life only." So they give all of their time and thought and attention to this world and leave out all thought for the world which is to come. This is spiritual suicide. This is folly at its worst. This is the way men condemn themselves to eternal death. And yet all the while God has done and is doing everything necessary to save men and bring them home to Glory.

First, a man climbs over the mountain of the Church, then he climbs over the mountain of Gospel sermons, then he climbs over the mountain of God's great Book, then he climbs over the mountain of his conscience, then he climbs over the mountain of better judgment, then he climbs over the mountain of a mother's love and prayers and tears, then he climbs over the mountain of the sorrows and shadows of life, then he climbs over the mountain of God's Holy Spirit.

Finally, he comes to Calvary. There he sees the very dying form of One who died for him. Caring not for that death, he climbs over Jesus Christ and goes down to an everlasting death. But he should not live and die like this. Heaven is sure and hell is sure and between the two there is an impassable gulf. A man ought to get on Christ's side today, so that he will be on His side of that gulf throughout all eternity.

Some years ago I was holding a meeting in a certain church. On Thursday night a young man came to me after the service, telling me that he would like to talk to me. I saw the tears standing in his eyes. I saw the deep note of conviction written upon his face. I knew that his heart had been touched in the service that evening. I took him over to a little Sunday school room just off the main auditorium. As soon as I closed the door, he fell down upon his knees and began to weep. After a little while I was able to point him to the Saviour, and when he left the church that night he was rejoicing in Christ; he had been born again through repentance and faith in the Lord. A week later he came to me and said, "Do you know what day this is?" I answered, "Yes, it is Thursday. What about it?" Then he said to me, "One week ago tonight I gave my heart to Christ. I have found more joy and more happiness in this one week than I have known in all the other twenty-four years of my life."

My friend, it can be even so with you. He offers you everything good for this world and for the world to come. Why not give your heart to Christ today? When you come down to the end of the way and when you look back over your life, you will be sorry for many things you have done, but you will never be sorry that you gave your heart to Christ and joined His church and lived your life for Him. You have everything to gain and nothing to lose.

Oh, come today, and rest in the salvation which He wrought for you on Calvary's Cross. Come, just as you are, and let Him save you. Come and let Him give you the best things of earth and the best things of heaven.

Scripture Index